C.L. LAWRENCE

Fallon House Publishers, LLC
New Jersey

International Standard Book Number
ISBN- 978-09972082 52
Printed in the United States of America

DEDICATED TO

MY AWFULLY AWESOME DAUGHTER
Alexis Fallon Medley

"Miss Prissy"
You're everything I wish I was at her age.

&

MY AWFULLY AWESOME COUSIN

Fondra Marie Fontenot

July 24, 1950 - February 24, 2017

The first Awfully Awesome person in my life

Download your FREE eBook @
LawrenceMinistries.com
C.L. LAWRENCE
DO YOU!
YOU ARE
ANOINTED
TO BE YOU

CONTENTS

CONTENTS

ACKNOWLEDGMENTS

My Hallelujah, as always, goes to God first for pouring new ideas into my mind daily, trusting me with thoughts and ventures outside the box, and for bringing awfully awesome people into my life who encourage me in my ordered steps.

I'm happy to mention just a few people who've inspired me in their unique ways. Michael David Medley, who, at five years old, said: "Mommy you can't be afraid to try new things." From that day until this, his words have given me the stone I've needed when the Goliath of doubt stood in my way.

I'm grateful for Jonathan Medley, my roadie. If you had to choose the last person with whom to be on earth, choose Jonathan. He makes life an unforgettable adventure.

I'm grateful to Rev. Roland Cooper, for being my bridge across the generation gap of communication, teaching me to translate my thoughts into cyber-speak. Thanks Coop.

I'm grateful to Brenda Harper-Davis, who, in the eye of the Euroclydon, she's there saying "We'll get through this." When nothing's happening, she says, "Something's happening." Thanks Brenda for always being right. well, almost always.

INTRODUCTION

We have everything we need to be all that God has created us to be. The Bible says that God has given us everything that pertains to life and Godliness (2 Peter 1:3). God put his awesome in us, so, we already have the tools necessary to be amazing in the Kingdom of God. Sometimes we need to do a little tweaking here and there, or, perhaps, be reminded of a few things. Timothy tells us to stir up the gift that's within us (2 Timothy 1:6). That means it's already there. Once we get a glimpse through the Word of what God has created in us from the beginning, the Holy Spirit will have something to work with. He'll impart the confidence you need to never again ask permission to be who you know you are deep down inside.

We've all looked at awesome people, however you define awesome, and wondered how they knew how to do what they did to be, for example, "successful." They seem to just have it all together. You've watched and admired them because they've got something but how did they get it. Were they born with it? You wonder what they know and how they know it. Who told them how to be awesome. What's their secret?

Awesome people, amazing people, successful people share commonalities that cause them to stand out. They have discipline, perhaps not in every area of their lives but in certain things. For example:

- They're always on time; never late
- They do the things other people won't do
- They arrive early and don't mind staying late
- They don't watch the clock and focus on the hours; they focus on getting the job done
- They dare to think in fresh, new ways
- They seek different perspectives
- Their decision-making process is multifaceted in the scope of considering varied dynamics

- They don't play the blame game, but take responsibility for their actions and decisions
- They know themselves well enough to know what trips them up or causes them to stumble
- They do due diligence; homework on people and situations

A secret is something unknown until someone lets you in on it. Well, this book lets you in on the top ten secrets of ordinary people with mindsets, practices, and mantras active on the inside that reflect awesomeness on the outside.

As a Christian writer, I make references to scripture and there's "faith talk" throughout, but this book isn't about the sinlessness of awesome people, for obviously there are no such creatures. It's about ten things that will set you apart from others; causing the awesome already on the inside to bubble up on the outside. These secrets are the sacrifice and investment required for personal growth beyond the average, professionalism beyond the level of mediocrity, and cultivating the seeds of personal empowerment; tidbits of wisdom that bridge the gap between ordinary and extraordinary; and give you the missing pieces taken for granted, but that make the difference you're looking for in your life.

Read every secret, then go be awesome!

Awesome People
KEEP IT REAL

Keep It REAL

R

RELEASE THE PAST
Forgive sins. Travel light in the peace and good thoughts God has in his plan for your life.

... this one thing I do, forgetting those things which are behind, and reaching forth unto those things which are before,
Philippians 3:13

E

EMBRACE THE NOW
Appreciate the blessings in the now & the beauty in the moment. The now moment is all we have.

This is the day that the Lord has made We will rejoice and be glad in it.
Psalm 118:24

A

ACKNOWLEDGE GOD
You represent someone greater than yourself; a purpose grander than your own. You're an integral part of a divine plan that began in eternity past, transcending the now, extending into eternity future.

[4] So shalt thou find favor and good understanding in the sight of God and people.
[5] Trust in the LORD with all thine heart; and lean not unto thine own understanding. [6] In all thy ways acknowledge him, and he shall direct thy paths.
Proverbs 3:4-6

L

LEAN INTO THE FUTURE.
LEAN GODWARD
Put your weight on it. LOOK straight ahead; stay focused to avoid distractions. We move toward what we see, on that which we focus our attention.

[13] ... reaching forward to those things which are ahead,
[14] I press toward the goal for the prize of the high calling of God in Christ Jesus.
Philippians 3:13, 14

NOTES

You are fearfully &
wonderfully made.

Psalm 139:14

Secret # 1

You're Already Awesome!!!

Yes! YOU ARE. YOU MAY THINK NOT, but you are, and you're going to get lots of proof. Hmmm, ok, so there probably aren't many people who would say, "I am awesome." A safe assumption is, you're one of those people. You may say it of others and really mean it but when it comes to yourself, you wouldn't own it personally. Is that you? That's ok. Stay with me, I've got evidence; chapter and verse.

Most can quickly and easily delineate faults, weakness, shortcomings, bad habits, shameful indiscretions; and no problem at all with acknowledging physical areas they consider unattractive in themselves. But – to flip the script and give equal time to the positive things and attractiveness in themselves; never. You may not be terribly offended if others say you're awesome but you'd never say it about yourself, not even when you're home alone looking in the mirror at your awesome self.! There, I said it for you again. *You are awesome!*

Still not convinced? Think for a moment of all you've been through. Broken dreams, betrayal, loss of love or loss of a loved one, illness, struggle through school, mental illness, domestic violence, divorce, and the list goes on. Remember when you thought you couldn't take anymore, when you thought you couldn't make it another day, when things were so bad you thought God didn't love you. We've all been there; and if you haven't, just live a little longer because no one gets through this life without pain and struggle of some kind. The Hallelujah is you made it. You're holding this book so that proves you made it another day. You're still standing. You may not know how you made it without losing your mind, but you made it. You may have scars, but you're here. You may be wet from the storm, but you're here. No matter what life has thrown at you, you're still here and your very presence is a testimony that you're awesome because God put his awesome in you.

God put his awesome in you

In fairness to those who fall into the populace who deny almost anything good about themselves, it's understandable considering the value placed on humility. Most people wouldn't want to be thought of as a narcissist, boastful, or cocky. Certainly, it isn't the intent of this discussion to encourage you into vainglorious self-perception, but there is room to accept what God thinks of you without crossing the boundary into the AOE (Association of Egomaniacs). The Bible, the ultimate authority, is the only credible lens through which one can see themselves clearly. The Bible says we're fearfully and wonderfully made. It's interesting that the Complete Jewish Bible (CJB) translates the word fearfully to awesomely. Beyond the wonder of the amazing human body with all its intricacies and moving parts, there's still more. The "more" is that which makes you, you. From the human vantage point we'd consider such things as personality, character, intellect, talents, spiritual gifts, etc., but from the perspective of the Word of God, there is infinitely more.

Everything has a beginning. Everything starts somewhere, including you. We meet the world at the point of human existence, at birth. God was there in active participation at your earthly birth.[a] It's exciting that God would think you important enough to be present when you came into the world. David said it beautifully when he wrote,

> *When I consider thy heavens, the work of thy fingers, the moon and the stars, which thou hast ordained. What is man, that thou art mindful of him, and the son of man, that thou visitest him? For thou hast made him a little lower than the angels, and hast crowned him with glory and honour.*[b]

Now, look at the verse again with the translation contemporized, and personalized.

> When I look at your heavens, the work of your fingers, the moon, and stars that you set in place, what am I but a mere mortal (man or woman), that you concern yourself with me, and watch over me with such care? You made me a little lower than the angels, crowned me with glory and honor. You've given me rule over what your hands made and put everything under my feet.

To get what God has for you to know in his Word, you have to take the time to put yourself into it and make it personal. Use I, me, mine; put your name in it. It's okay to do that because the Word was written to you and for you. To get the mind of God, you must wear the scripture as your garment, step into the scripture and be there listening and digesting what God has to say to you, for you, and about you.

Your birth was not your beginning. When sperm met egg, that was not your beginning. Your beginning was in the mind of God, in the imagination of God. He imagined you, then created what he imagined. Think about it. God created what he imagined. Then he chose you to be in Christ before the

---

[a] Psalm 22, 9, 10, 11; 71:6; 134:13; Galatians 1:15

[b] Psalm 8:3-5

foundation of the world.[c] To be chosen you had to exist. If you were chosen then among all that did exist, there must be something in you that's worthwhile now. Think further about your creation. God doesn't make errors, faux pas, bloopers, or blunders. He has a plan that spans through to eternity future. Everything he creates is part of his plan and has a purpose in the plan. Plans require thought. That's what a plan is, the result of careful and meticulous thought. When it comes to you, the Bible says, God's thoughts are for good and not of evil, with an expected good outcome.[d] Sometimes that's all you need to hear.

You are your own unique brand

You can see already how you're awesome, right? There will never be another you. You aren't a duplicate of anyone else. You may look like your mother; or look like your father; or look like your twin, but you are uniquely you, The Designer's original, one of a kind, distinctive in every way. There isn't, nor will there ever be another you. The sound of your voice is yours. The way you walk is your walk. The way you talk is you. You are your own brand. Awesome, authentically, unmistakably you. Celebrate your brand. Your relationship with God, your gifts, talents, and anointing gives you access to the power to release the awesomeness of God that he formed, then breathed in you.

Awesome Authentically Unmistakably You

There'll always be those who plant and cultivate seeds of doubt, causing you to doubt yourself. They have their purpose and we'll get to that shortly. The traditional counsel would be to not allow anyone to make you doubt yourself, and certainly that is the goal; but let's look at doubt planters through the story of Dancing with the Bumble Bee.

---

[c] Ephesians 1:4
[d] Jeremiah 29:11

Dancing with the Bumble Bee

Planters of doubt are like bumble bees in summertime, always buzzing around. There you are, shower fresh, great cologne, aftershave, or perfume, dressed in bright colors reflecting your colorful you, and here they come, uninvited, buzzing around bothering you with the threat of their sting. As soon as you get rid of one, here comes another. To say, don't let the doubters cause you to doubt would be like saying don't let the presence of the bumble bee bother you. They bother you because you know what they can do. To varying degrees the presence of the bumble bee sends most of us into a nervous terror with flailing arms and awkward movements, later hoping no one witnessed our dance with the bumble bee.

Consider this. You never see a bumble bee buzzing around poop. They're attracted to what's fresh, clean, sweet, and bright. That's you. (Now, it's up to you to deal with the bumble bee. This is just to point out why they buzz around you.) Understanding why the nay sayers and doubters are attracted to you is important, but what's more important to understand is the presence of the bumble bee can cause you to hurt yourself even if it never stings you. Your nervous, frightened, uncontrolled reactions can cause you to fall or hurt yourself in some way. As for the bumble bee, well, it flies away to terrify some other unsuspecting soul.

Moral of the Story: People that make you doubt yourself are like bumble bees. You'll never get rid of them all, so figure out how to handle yourself in the dance.

Think Fresh

Start now, this day, this moment; think in new ways. Take a fresh look at old assumptions. Nothing will happen to you if you try it. No flaming sword will come from the sky if you ponder new thoughts and ideas. The aim isn't to think differently just to think differently, but to stretch your capacity for thought, allowing greater insights from God to enter in and give you a greater view of God's grace. The Bible places heavy emphasis on the mind and your responsibility of its use and expected end. Transformation is achieved by the renewing of the mind.[e] Renewing your mind, changing the way you think leads to changing yourself for the better. Benjamin Disrael says, "Nurture your mind with great thoughts, for you will never go any higher than you think." The Apostle Paul makes two strong life changing statements; one a statement of fact, the other an imperative, both powerfully transformational in their practical application.

Start now
This day
This moment

1. *"Let this mind be in you, which was also in Christ Jesus."*[f] If you know Jesus, the man, try to imagine the way he thought and assume his mindset as your own. You cannot be negative, judgmental, and harmfully critical in the way you see people, including yourself. When anyone had an encounter with Jesus, their lives were made better. They were either healed physically, mentally, or spiritually; freed from a captive existence of blindness, or narrowmindedness, or freed from the imprisonment of their own mind. Stepping into the mindset of Jesus will elevate one to a personal level

[e] Romans 12:2
[f] Philippians 2:5

always for the better. Take a fresh look and release the awesome in you that you didn't know was there.

2. "*But we have the mind of Christ,*[g]" which is to say that we're guided and directed by his thoughts and purposes. What an amazing gift, to have the mind of Christ. We don't have to read a book on an issue, watch a talk show or consult with others as confused as we may be. We have the mind of Christ and the Holy Spirit can bring the voice of Christ's mind into our consciousness. It just doesn't get any better than that.

Awfully Awesome people think differently. They don't discredit the conventional wisdom, but inside their heads, they step outside the box. They ask questions, "Is there anything else to consider?" "Before I close the case, is there anything else to consider or study that could make a positive difference?" "Can I spin this negative in a positive direction?' "How can I make this negative work for me rather than against me?" This is challenging until learning to think in new ways becomes a habit.

Is There Really a Box?

Yes, indeed there is, and it's a good box. It holds history and traditions, standards and boundaries, blueprints for life, values, and answers to questions. In fact, it's a perfect little box, perfectly comfortable to the extent of its dimensions and content. In the world, there are three kinds of people:

1. **Inside the Box People**:

   Most people are Inside the Box people. Inside the Box people fit inside the box and live in it quite comfortably. They can't think or comprehend anything outside the box so their thoughts never venture outside of their

[g] Corinthians 2:16b

comfort zone, for to do so stirs conflict with the nature of the way they think and process the world. They're happy that way and that's fine. Some may try but they quickly retreat with the thought that Outside the Box isn't acceptable.

2. **Outside the Box People**:

   These are those who say, wait a second, start asking questions, testing assumptions and challenging things inside the box. They mean absolutely no harm. It's just the way their mind works. Imagine that they step outside of the box and look around. They respect the contents and don't try to empty it. They just walk around the box and look at things from every vantage point. That's how they discover new ideas, different views and find fresh perspectives they can use and share with others. These are Outside the Box thinkers who can traverse inside and outside the box comfortably and seamlessly.

3. **No Box People**:

   There are indeed some who appear to think there is no box. They're usually the precious artistically gifted people in the Kingdom of God. For them, there may in fact, be no box. They aren't lawless, rule breakers, or renegades. They see the world through unencumbered eyes, simplistic values; processing and communicating with the world they see as unnecessarily complicated.

Each one, indispensable to the beauty of the human tapestry. Which one are you? So important to pause and figure that out in order to resolve insecurities you may have. You would be amazed at how many kinks in your life would be straightened with just the resolution of understanding the orientation of your thought processes.

Cultivators of Doubt Have a Purpose

Those who plant seeds of doubt, even unintentionally, can cause you to feel insecure. When a person is insecure in who they are, or what they're doing, they find themselves asking permission to be themselves; seeking approval and affirmation for who they are, and the thoughts and ideas that God has poured into them to take them to the next level of becoming who he created them to be. How many times have you had a good idea and allowed someone to talk you out of it, or pondered their questions until you doubted so much that you dismissed the idea only to see, later, someone else run with it and make a success of it? Most of the people who offer doubt and criticism have no real accomplishments of their own, no expertise in the area of which they're criticizing you, but, they talk and you listen. Stop talking to the devil. Stop listening to the voices of the enemy. If God gives you an idea, your next step is to do the homework on it, consult with those whom God has brought into your space as a result of your prayers. More about that in Secret # 6, Choose Wisely Your Inner Circle.

People who cause doubt actually have a purpose in your life. Just as you have a purpose, so do they. Their purpose is to help you get to that expected end Jeremiah talks about. That seems totally crazy. The ones who offer affirmation and encouragement are the helpers – and they are! We welcome them into our lives and thank God for them. But the people that cause you to doubt encourage you in a different but essential way. They cause questions to bubble up on the inside. Questions let you know what kind of personal power you have because questions demand answers. You must do something with a question; either answer it or ignore it. That's a personal power choice. Ignoring it is doing something with it just as is the choice to answer the question, so don't get upset with questions. Doubt brings you to a place of question and decision. You either quit in discouragement, or you examine yourself and what you're doing, and keep it moving. Re-examination is always good. It makes you better, sharper, stronger, wiser, and ready for the next round. Doubters position you to catch your own mistakes so you can fix them. The nay sayers and doubt mongers take you from awesome to awfully awesome being totally unaware of how God is using them to push you into your purpose and destiny.

Nay sayers and doubters have a purpose

The word and concept of destiny is a much-used term and rightfully so. Destiny means purpose, intention, calling. Destiny means you have something to do, some place to go, there's an end game. Along the way there will be distractions, hurdles, obstacles in the form of situations and people. Situations and circumstances can be huge but people often cause you the most trouble; people with little annoyances. What do you do with those people who assume it to be their life mission to just frustrate others? They are so in need of attention in any way they can get it. Awesome people are creative so you must find creative ways to deal with people without doing damage to them. On the next page, there's a funny but true story called, "Throw a Dog a Bone," that makes the point about creative ways of dealing with annoying people that won't go away. Before you read the story, consider these questions:

1. Who's in your world planting seeds of doubt.
2. Focus past their annoyance and think of why they might be in your life. What might their purpose be? Is it to make you think creatively? Is it to build your tolerance?
3. Are they planting doubt because they lack the courage and faith you have?
4. They will not change so you must change your perspective of them, and response to them.
5. What can you do to divert them without hurting them?

Throw a Dog a Bone

In the neighborhood where I grew up, there was a dog named Kelly. Kelly was the dog from hell. He was about the size of a half grown German Shepherd, never on a leash and seemed never to be in his owners house. He was always on the street harassing kids on their way to and from school and people on their way to and from the bus stop. He would bark at everyone, snap at their heels and run. He almost seemed to laugh at the frustration he was causing day after day.

One night, we had chicken for dinner, and I got an idea. I put a chicken bone in my pocket. The next morning like clockwork there was Kelly, hiding in the hedges, waiting to lunge out and terrorize the next passerby, and so he did. About half way to the bus stop I threw the chicken bone in his direction. It was amazing. That demon dog immediately turned, completely forgetting about me and everyone else. He went after that meatless bone like it was a T-bone steak. It did exactly what I hoped it would do; got an annoying dog off my heels.

Moral of the story: Throw the dog a bone. Keep a pocket full of bones. When folks are annoying you, throw them a bone. Doesn't need to have meat on it. They don't require meet. Just give them something to chew on and they'll leave you alone.

NOTES

NOTES

Being yourself is simply
bringing your treasure to the world;
your color to the rainbow.

– C.L. Lawrence

Secret # 2

Be Your Authentic Self

IF YOU WERE CHARGED WITH IDENTITY theft; would the charges stick? Think for a moment. Are you being your real self? Do you know? The question has nothing to do with wigs, toupees, cosmetic enhancements, or anything related to outward appearance. Those things are your choices, adornments that change with styles and fashion. Your authentic self is what lives vibrantly through or lies silently beneath what's visible. Authenticity means genuine; real; not false or copied. What was first, at the root, the core? What was there before anything else ever was? Authenticity, then, begins with who God created you to be; who you are on the inside. Your authentic self is the genuine you, not a copy of someone else, who you look like or what you do for a living. Your authentic self is your unique you, who you are, your passions, values, what you think, how you think, how you process and interact with the world, your personality, temperament, and disposition. Your authenticity begins with God.

Are you a patient person? A tolerant person? A compassionate person? Are you free spirited, comfortable with ambiguity, or do you prefer structure? Are you an "inside the box" or an "outside the box" person? Are you laid back or assertive? Are you a nine to five person or do you work until the job is done? Do you naturally take the lead in situations even without the title? The questions can go on and on. There is no subliminal judgement in any of the questions, no good or bad, right or wrong. Everyone is different; everyone is valid in their personality, style; their created being. Every person is a creative expression of God's image, each reflecting parts of the infinite facets of God's self.

There are several instruments,[h] personality theories and psychometrics tests models which define personality types, work styles, leadership styles, etc. While you don't want to get bogged down or obsessed with the instruments, they're helpful in a couple of ways. While not culturally objective, they present an outline of the personality and leadership styles, giving you a larger view of the array of types and where you may theoretically find your definition. Consistent with your level of open-mindedness, engaging in the instruments can be intimidating or informative. Have fun with them. They're not meant to be conclusive, only thought provoking. Approach them broadmindedly, without preconceived notions and that will decrease the element of judgement and bias normally brought to an experience. View the results as a guide or a window through which to gain insight into yourself. No one, except God, knows you better than you do. Personality and work style instrument often help you to get to know yourself a little better.

---

[h] The Four Temperaments/Four Humours, Carl Jung's Psychological Types, Myers Briggs® personality types theory (MBTI® model), Keirsey's personality types theory (Temperament Sorter model), Hans Eysenck's personality types theory, Katherine Benziger's Brain Type theory, William Moulton Marston's DiSC personality theory (Inscape, Thomas Int., etc.) Belbin Team Roles and personality types theory, The 'Big Five' Factors personality model, FIRO-B® Personality Assessment model, The Birkman Method®, Lumina Spark, Morphopsychology

Secondly, it's important to have a general understanding of your personality type. It goes a long way in learning to accept and appreciate yourself, the person God created. It also helps in the understanding of the unique ways in which the Holy Spirit guides and uses you in the Kingdom of God. Consider for a moment, Spiritual Gifts.[i] Paul takes time to talk about spiritual gifts and the precision of their operation. Insight reveals that while different personality types operate in each of the gifts, there are certain personality types more suited for certain gifts. Being your authentic self, the self who God created in you positions you to function with excellence in your respective spiritual gift(s) and calling.

Being your authentic self is living from the inside out, interacting with the world through the lens and grid of who you really are. Who you are on the inside has nothing to do with what others are thinking or saying about you. Your authentic self is the "you" who never changes. You may hide your you, disguise your you, or even try to kill your you by trying to be someone else, but your authentic self will always be there waiting for affirmation and opportunities for expression. There is a need for the real you in the world or God would not have bothered to create you if you weren't somehow necessary in his overall eternal plan. You have a voice that only certain one's can hear. You have a style that only certain ones can relate to. You have "a way" that only certain ones will follow. Paul says, God will supply all our needs. You are the need of someone or something in God's plan. Start wrapping your mind around that thought. No, you're not the "itness of the allness," or the "end all to be all," but recognizing the intentionality of your being is the perfect place to begin. God, our creator, uniquely designed every person. He wasn't having a bad day when he came up with

To come to the life experience unpretentiously is a choice

[i] I Corinthians 12

your blueprint. You're not a mistake, an "OOPS!" or afterthought, substitute, or an addendum, but part of the divine tapestry of time, the bigger picture, set in motion before the foundation of the world. You have a specific purpose, a strategic part, a role to play in the drama of eternity, but to see the beauty of it all you must come unpretentiously to the life experience. It's a choice.

It isn't an easy choice because there is the matter of wanting to be accepted. There is a cultural habit of comparing one's self to others; against biased standards of beauty; socially defined definitions of success and accomplishment; against others who've reached a level of celebrity or notoriety to which one may admire or aspire. At an early age, well-meaning voices dictate what to think of yourself, what the world thinks of you, what to think of the world around you and how to fit into it, … or not. Nurturing, social grooming, mentoring is good and necessary, and you're blessed when it comes from those who love and desire to see you grow into your best self. Be aware, however, there are other voices eager to be heard, shaping your perceptions with the fruit of their life experience of narrow vision, dwarfed goals, and sight walking. Rhetoric that constructs walls around you, giving you a box to live in, fostering a world view limited to their own.

Sound bites, highway billboards, overt and covert messages coming at you every minute of the day telling you how you ought to look, how you should think and feel, what you should buy, and what/who you ought to be. Carefully crafted marketing strategies using subliminal suggestions that feed your demons of destructive self-images, self-hatred, self-doubt, and low self-esteem plant the seeds of inadequacy watered with doubt, artfully conspiring to convince you, first, that there is a problem, and, secondly, that the problem is "You." You're not good enough. You need to be a better you, a more appealing you, a more successful you. You're too much of this or not enough of that, but there's a solution just for you that will bring you to that subjective standard of "perfection." The message is clear: You aren't good enough as you are. You need to be fixed. Truth is not the measure and reality is not the issue. Keeping you focused outwardly is the means to prevent you from seeing inwardly, blinding you to your inner treasure and the beauty of your authentic self.

Many spend their lifetime trying to find someone else to be, copying this one and mimicking that one, thinking someone else is somehow better. So deeply rooted that it becomes second nature to look outwardly for the solution to becoming "the better you." So much a part of your sub consciousness that you pass it down to your children. So engrained in your psyche that you judge yourself and others by the perceptions continuously cultivated in your mind over your lifetime.

Many spend a lifetime trying to find someone else to be.

It's no wonder precious people of God lose their sense of themselves long before ever having an opportunity to become aware of their true selves and appreciate who they are as a wonderful, planned creation of God with a divine purpose and an intentional future. You are anointed to be you. You're your own worst critic, finding what you perceive as flaws in yourself, even sometimes asking God why he made you this way. You certainly aren't the first to ask that question.[i] BUT! to whom are you comparing yourself? Against whose standard are you measuring yourself? Certainly, you should smooth edges and rid yourself of destructive behaviors and habits that masquerade as second nature. You should stir up and perfect your gifts and talents, but surely not change who you are. You're not approved

You are anointed to be you

---

[i] Romans 9:20 Nay but, O man, who art thou that repliest against God? Shall the thing formed say to him that formed it, Why hast thou made me thus?

because you're perfect, you're approved because of to whom you belong. To be your authentic self you have to know your you, and accept yourself as a good product of God's work that day; the reality of his imagination, perfect imperfections, flaws and all. Whatever you are, too much of this and not enough of that, you are perfectly shaped and fashioned to do what you were created to do. You aren't too short, too tall, too fat, too thin, too shy, too outspoken. You're of the right race, the right socio-economic location. "It's a man's world." ***News Flash!*** It isn't a man's world; it's God's world. So step up and be that woman God created you to be and don't apologize for it. "It's hard being a man." ***News Flash!*** It's hard being human. Get over it. Get on with life. There are people waiting for you.

The desire to matter, fit in, be accepted, have recognition, a sense of purpose and belonging is very strong, leading you to become unduly influenced, giving up your capacity of pure, free, independent thought to the degree necessary to feel accepted and affirmed. Using a grassroots term, that's "selling yourself cheap." When you relinquish your power of self-validation to others, adapting yourself to what you think you should be without giving yourself the benefit of seeking to know and cultivate the person God has created you to be; without a positive, healthy, and confident self-awareness, you will seek to be someone else; a copycat; a fraud. No! No! No! That's ***Identity Theft.*** A stolen, even borrowed identity, won't last. To find value in being someone else is an insult to your authentic self, as well as the God who made you.

You may be inspired by others and try to develop similar qualities of character, but those qualities will be expressed through your own person. When you're content with yourself, comfortable in your own skin, you don't compare or compete with others. You can look with admiration at others, their accomplishments, and elevations, hear the accolades and applause, and be genuinely happy for them without feeling slighted or passed over. It's in the knowing that "what God has for you is for you. It's in knowing your spiritual gifts and calling, passion and purpose that allows you to rise above the low state of envy and jealousy because you know who you are in Christ. When you're not trying to be something or someone you're not, there's an incredible peace that abides on the inside, and rest from having to be "on" all the time.

What is your authentic self?

"I am nobody but myself." - Ralph Ellison

When you set yourself free to be yourself, you never have to think about how to be yourself. You just do what comes naturally. Do you! Do it the way you do it. Say it the way you say it. Sing it the way you sing it. Play it the way you play it. Think the way you think. If you have a question, ask it. It you have a suggestion, share it. If it doesn't make sense, say it. "Free to be me" isn't that philosophy of hedonism, self-indulgence, pleasure seeking humanism or taking license to be lawless. Being yourself is simply bringing your treasure to the world; your color to the rainbow. Don't let the nay sayers intimidate you with criticism when you're trying to be your authentic self. "Free to be me" is a mental posture that allows the one liberty to grow into what God would have you to be, and finding the internal peace and freedom in being that which is you.

Children get it, but somewhere along the way, lose it. Listen to the funny but insightful wisdom in an exchange between three children as one teases and mimicks the other:

Lex: *Don't copy me!*

Nip: But you're so cute.

Lex: *I know, but you don't get to be cute by being a copycat.*

Nip: OK, then how did you get so cute?

Lex: *God made me that way. That's how.*

Nip: How can I get cute like you?

Lex: *You can't get cute like me, Boo. You have to get cute like you. That's the way God works.*

Dove: That's right, and God made me cuter than you both.

Your authentic self is your "cute." It's your "you;" your unique you. You know when you've found your cute when you can say, I'm okay with me. I'm comfortable with me. I like me. "*For as he thinketh in his heart, so is he.*"[k]:

Authenticity is an easy concept to entertain when talking about artwork or antiques; but not so easy in the context of self and on the very personal level of self-examination. What does the real you look like? What makes you uniquely you? Even the thought of engaging in self-exploration to answer those questions can be quite intimidating. You don't know what or who you might find. Suppose "I don't like what I find?" Ok, that's an understandable fear. Remember, everything starts with God. In Genesis chapter one, in the beginning of all creation, as God completed the various entities it tells us that he saw that "it was good." Say it with me, "I'm the manifestation of God's creative imagination." When he finished creating you, he saw that you were good. He likes what he did. He loves you. The Holy Spirit will guide you to a new and true vision of yourself as you make finding, accepting and being your authentic self an intentional part of your spiritual development.

---

[k] Proverbs 23:7

What does authenticity have to do with anything?

Authenticity has to do with everything. You speak before you say a word. Authenticity speaks with a loud voice. It attracts others. People are drawn to those who are comfortable in their own skin. Others feel comfortable and secure in your self-confidence. If you're masquerading as someone else, perhaps a person you admire or one whose success you desire, then you're always acting, never being.

The absence of authenticity brings everything about you into question. Do your beliefs and philosophies drawn breath in your spirit first? Or are you repeating what you've heard or what's been passed down. If the perception of you begins before you say a word, then everything about you is an introduction of who you are. Your style. Is it you? Or are you copying someone else? Your speech. Is it you? Or are you mimicking someone else? Your delivery. Is it you? Or are you channeling someone else? Are you living out the uniqueness within yourself.? God never meant for you to be the same as any other or he could have created clones. God created all things, distinction in all things and beauty in the distinction. What is your distinction? What makes you distinctively, authentically you?

What is your distinction?

What makes you distinctively, authentically you?

Your personality, your approach to life in general, largely determines what you look for in life and what you'll get out of life. Some things you just can't fake no matter how hard you try. You may imitate someone's style, their persona, physical expressions, voice inflections, even little idioms but imitation becomes transparent over time, if not immediately to some..

You can't speak with authenticity what you don't believe, what you don't embrace within yourself. You may give sound to the words but you can't fake authenticity and without authenticity there is no real you. In other words, a negative, grumpy person can't speak about joy with any degree of spiritual integrity. No one would believe them. A judgmental person will have difficulty talking about the blessedness of God's outpouring of grace and favor, and the gift of salvation because judgmental people want you to pay for your sins and wear your sorrow. Judgmental, self-righteous people feel lifted when they bring others down.

If you're an old fohggy, fuddy duddy, who holds onto the way things used to be (and you can be that at 35 years old), you can't talk about the new things waiting in an exciting new future. You can't talk about Isaiah 42:9 or 43:19. How can you embrace the tools of technology, and social media if you're holding fast to the past? You can't talk about what you can't embrace. You can't talk about what you don't have in you because the thinly veiled façade soon breaks down. Authenticity or the lack thereof speaks with a loud voice and you completely unaware of it.

Finding Your Own Voice

Whether you're a public speaker, a writer, a radio personality, or none of the above, if you're alive and have an intelligent opinion about what's going on in life, then you have a voice. Not the voice that speaks for others necessarily, but more particularly, the voice that speaks for you. Your voice begins with God. Voice in this context isn't the audible sound that comes out of your mouth when you speak; it isn't volume or decibels. Your voice is your interpretations; the result of that which flows through your unique grid system on its way to becoming speech. Your voice begins with you in the Potter's hand; God molding and distinctively creating not just the vessel but the way the vessel receives, digests thoughts and feels. You're recognizable by what you say and how you say it. Your voice is distinctive. It's your signature. It's the sound of your personality, your personalized way of interpreting things and presenting them. Your voice reflects your passions, gifts, that about which you care deeply, the totality of your life experiences; your testimonies, and the wisdom you've gained from your joys and sorrows; so much so that the Holy Spirit can use any or all of it to empower the words you share with others. Your voice is what makes your aura particular, and alive.

The Bible says in both accounts of the Gospel, Matthew, and Luke, that what comes out of our mouths is that which is in our heart. Subconsciously or not, we run thoughts and concepts through our personal grid systems and what comes out has a little or a lot of ourselves woven into our conversations. Are there "grace notes" in the melody of your speech or are you condescending and critical.[1] Watch out for people who are negative and critical of others, always putting others down. Don't be that person. Be that person who lifts people up, encourages others, finds good in others. If you're not like that then practice until your "voice" is a blessing to others, consequently a blessing to yourself as well.

The buzz word is "brand." Your voice is your brand. Is your voice familiar even to you? How would you describe your brand? If your life could speak, what would it say? What are you known for in the kingdom realm? Are you known as a person who listens, shares wisdom, affirmation of what God has done in others; one who speaks humbly and transparently from good and bad experiences? Or, are you a rapper, a hollow sound like the echo from an empty cavern. If you were an instrument, which one would it be and how would you sound? Poignant questions yet many exhaust themselves hiding in someone else's

---

[1] Read Secret # 7, "Watch Your Mouth"

brand, never asking the questions. Be bold. Ask the questions, then take the time to answer yourself.

What do I think about this or that? My opinions, the things I espouse and express; are they what I believe or what's been passed down to me or I've heard from others? Is it what my mind, my spirit, and my emotions have discussed with the scriptures? Do I know my own mind? Does this really sound like me?

Finding your voice means discovering your comfort zone, the courage to give full expression in your thoughts and conversations through your true self. It's about the story you tell (conversation) and how you tell it (voice). When you think of your voice, think of your purpose. Is it to motivate, inspire, teach, challenge, comfort encourage, empower, …? Your purpose will come through in your conversations. No one can say things the way you say them. No one can feel the meaning and express things the way you can.

Developing your authentic voice takes time, courage, and practice. It means overcoming the fear of being yourself and letting go of what others think. Sometimes you don't yet know what your true voice sounds like because you've been mimicking others for so long. It takes self-excavation, daring to discover what you have buried deep within, or what has been buried by any number of influences around you: culture, church, workplace, family. When you can understand that you have a voice that is exclusively yours to develop and to share, you'll stop allowing yourself to be diminished by mimicking the voice of others. You'll no longer define yourself in comparison to others or based on what others are doing or saying. The next time you feel yourself starting to compare yourself to others, **STOP!** Remind yourself that you have your own voice, unique to you, to your conversation, your destiny, and your calling.

Think of the five most successful people in America; a tech genius who changed the world of technology starting in his garage, a billionaire who didn't rip anyone off but just figured out how money works, religious leaders who've built great ministries marked with integrity; ordinary people who have done extraordinary things. They were not led by the nay saying voices outside of themselves. Instead they followed the voice God planted inside of them. When they speak you can hear it; not the sound, but the substance. You hear their passions, motivations, their soul satisfactions. When you speak, what do you hear? What do people hear?

On the day of Pentecost, Peter preached a to thousands of people. Each heard the Gospel in their own language. Of the thousands, the Bible says 3,000 were saved. Let's step out of the box and stretch our thoughts a little bit to see how that may apply within the framework of our concern. While there's one Holy Spirit, there's diversity within the body of Christ, the ear of the soul and the language the soul understands. It isn't a language you can study or learn. It's language that emanates from one's being. Just as teaching styles have been adapted to meet different learning styles, so God created you, unique in your language to resonate with the diversity of his hearers. Authenticity of self gives life to authenticity of voice. Your voice is your divine responsibility to God, yourself, and to others for whom you're meticulously designed to reach.

There are those who will only hear the good news of any kind, in the language of your speech, your voice. Not talking about the language of a nationality (African, French, German, …) but your language, that which is filtered through the wisdom gleaned from the testimony of your life journey. Your voice doesn't change your truth, but it changes how the story is told. It may include passion and compassion not experienced by others, yet which makes the story audible to someone who otherwise couldn't hear it. If you're a copycat, then all those whom you were created to bless when you interact with them will be robbed

Your voice is the supply of someone's need

of what was meant for them. God supplies every need. Your voice is the supply of someone's need.

There's no one else like you. There's a musical sound in you that is your own. A rhythm that emanates from your soul. A melody in the lyrics of your speech. The rhythm, the melody, and the lyrics create a symphonic language that is uniquely yours. It takes an emotionally secure, spiritually mature person to hear and appreciate their symphony and say within, I like the song born in my soul. When you hear it, that's when you've heard your own voice.

There's a melody in the lyrics of your speech

Let's revisit the question, "Do I know my own mind?" A question not to be answered hastily. The question is to suggest that you examine how you process the truths that lie before you and how you interpret matters in a time of change, in a world of broad exposure and intellectual access. Volumes can be written on how times have changed; how the world has changed.

Norms, values, beliefs, rules, ideologies, philosophies, continue to be challenged more quickly and dramatically than ever in the history of humanity. There is the thought, however, that things and people have not changed all that much. Cyberspace has created a global community exposing you to information previously unavailable. As a global citizen, you're exposed to information that sharpens your insight, expands your world view, and your thinking. That which existed without your knowledge is now in your personal space. You can no longer rest in the comfort of limited thoughts, experiences, and opinions, regurgitating what you've heard. So many, especially those in the generations in front of you, depend on your vision, your wisdom, your voice.

The information super highway has changed and challenged our reality on every level. Every belief is confronted and tested. The world will never be the same, and that's exciting. The prevailing thought or interpretations through the grid from years gone by may be too narrow for the larger landscape in which you now live. They may or may not be relevant or absolute in this regard: It may be conclusive based on the information available in a time and a particular social location. Yes, truth is what it is and does not change, but, revelation is God's prerogative. Be cautious of the arrogance to believe that in the breadth of your finite thinking; in the nanosecond of time you occupy in eternity, that you hold the complete volume of eternal truth. As time peels back layers of reality, a larger view brings greater light. That which was previously thought to be conclusive gives way to new considerations, new thoughts revelatory of a bigger and greater God.

You were created for this moment in history. You weren't born in the horse and buggy day, or the days of only snail mail and 10 cents per call phone booths on the street. You're in the age of technology. Silicon Valley has given the world tools never imagined even 20 years ago. The Internet has made it possible to experience new horizons, exposed diversity and challenges to faith and Christian values. That alone is God pealing back more layers of himself for you to experience. You can no longer relax in the comfort zone of neighborhood thinking; rest in the familiarity of limited thoughts, experiences, and opinions. The world is at your doorstep, in your living room, on the smart devices your children hold in their hands and the social networks with which no one can keep up.

You were created to reach and relate to a generation that no longer lives in the neighborhood but the world. You're on assignment to influence and impact the lives of others. Placed in this generation, directed to the awareness of the globalism and all the implications and applications. Things once hidden are now vying to be normative. What someone else thought about something may not be what resonates in that place where God speaks in your spirit.

You're trusted with the truth in the time in which you live. This isn't the norm of yesteryear, of "Ozzie & Harriet" or "Father Knows Best." Education, information, and social location, change thinking. No, you're not asked to change the truth but to give it a voice that's comprehensible. Examine and re-examine the challenges before you. It's not the conversation that needs to be changed because truth endures through all generations, but the voice God requires in such a time as this may be different. If may be yours. In the pursuit of your own voice, do you have the courage to accept the challenges to the things you've believed in and see what's left standing? There may be a difference in what you've been thinking when you were not in your authentic self. Have you the courage to give your own thoughts a second thought? Think about it.

Who do people say that I am?

Jesus and his disciples left Galilee and went up to the villages near Caesarea Philippi. As they were walking along, he asked them, "Who do people say I am?" Mark 8:27 NLT

Departing from the traditional interpretation of this scripture and using Jesus' question to illustrate a thought that can be extracted as a sub context, Jesus wasn't asking about the "buzz." He knew the people were talking about him, what they'd witnessed, what they'd heard and what they'd experienced. You can imagine with all he'd done; he would wonder how that translated in the people's minds. Were they "getting it?" He wasn't asking about what they thought of his deeds. He asked is disciples specifically not "what," but "who" the people were saying he was. Then he asked an even more poignant question, "Who do YOU say that I am?"

When Jesus was with the multitudes in the villages and on the outskirts of the cities he was healing and teaching. That was the perception of him some of the people had; healer, teacher. He was with his disciples day and night. They knew him up close and personal. He was asking if there was harmony between the man the people saw and the man the disciples knew; between his public persona and the man he was in his personal circle. Perhaps he was more concerned about who the disciples thought he was. Nevertheless, his question poses a sub context: Is everyone seeing the same thing? It takes a bit of courage to go there. Can people trust who/what they see? Authenticity is a matter of integrity. If you can't be who you are, your dependability is in question. Your words and actions won't stand the test of time and storm. Dare to think about it and ask yourself some questions. Who am I? Am I projecting my authentic self or a copy of someone else, or someone I've created in my imagination? Am I coming across the way I hope?

A person dissatisfied with their *self* will try to find someone else to be

To be your authentic self you must be well acquainted with your-self; accept your-self as a product of God's handiwork; perfections and perfect imperfections. Don't skip over this thought too quickly. To be acquainted with your-self is knowing your-self beneath the surface of what is, most often, thinly veiled. Think of yourself in practical terms, your personality, habits, tendencies, attitudes. Know your thoughts and intentions. Why do you do what you do? What moves and inspires you? What excites and motivates you? What makes your heart sing? Joy and sorrows. Are your emotions balanced? Anger. What are your triggers and how do you handle them? Are you vengeful? Do you honor commitments? Do you have friends? Is your moral compass in working order? Know you, the good you, the bad you, the ugly you, because, guess what! People know you. People see you and they react to the person they see, not the person you want or think they see.

Now, get a grip on your little self. Get your head on straight,[m] because an insecure person with difficulty accepting

[m] Secret # 3 Keep Your Head On Straight

him/herself, with a flawed sense of self-worth and unhealed wounds cannot be a true friend to anyone because they will use and abuse others to meet their own needs. A person dissatisfied with their self will try to find someone else to be.

Consider spiritual gifts, your natural gifts, skills, and talents, within the framework of this discussion. If you're unfamiliar with spiritual gifts or unsure of what gifts you have, it's worth taking the time to consult the readily available resources on the subject. You've been with yourself long enough to know your natural skills and talents, the things that come easily and effortlessly to you. Think of them in terms of being a part of a larger whole, the big picture of God's human tapestry. Positioning yourself in that framework will open your eyes as to how and where you fit in. You are who you are. You can be a better you, a more polished you, more perfected in your gifts, skills and abilities, but you can never be authentically someone else. You can impersonate or imitate but you cannot be someone else.

Who do people say you are? Can they trust what they see?

The question Jesus asked and that you must consider asking of yourself, "Who do people say that I am?" isn't to say that you are to be guided and conform to the opinions of others, but, to be used as a tool to see if you are being perceived as you know yourself to be. God created the authentic you. Through God's eyes, you're unmistakably you, redeemed, called, protected, ransomed, precious, honorable and loved in his sight.[n] Is that not enough to make you feel okay in your own skin? If you have doubts, keep reading. Secret #3 talks about how everything begins with God. When you start there, you understand God's intentionality in you included in the details of his eternal plan.

---

[n] Isaiah 43:1-7

Rabbi Zusya

(1718–1800)

Rabbi Zusya, an Orthodox rabbi and an early Hasidic luminary was renowned throughout the world for his insights as a scholar, teacher, and healer. When he was an old man he grew nervous as he thought about the world to come, his life and how little he had done. He began to imagine what the angel who would meet him might ask.

"Why were you not a Moses?" He thought, I shall answer with conviction, 'Because I was not born to be a Moses.' "And if the angel challenges me, 'But neither did you perform the feats of Elijah.' Again, he thought, I shall firmly respond, 'My mission was different from that of Elijah." But there is one question he feared God would ask and he'd be unable to answer: '

Why were you not a Rabbi Zusya?

Who do YOU say that YOU are?

Prayerfully Ponder

1. What's unique about you?

2. What are you known for?

3. What are your spiritual gifts? How do you use them?

NOTES

If

By Rudyard Kipling

IF YOU CAN KEEP YOUR HEAD WHEN ALL
ABOUT YOU ARE LOSING THEIRS and
blaming it on you,
If you can trust yourself when all men doubt you,
But make allowance for their doubting too;
If you can wait and not be tired by waiting,
Or being lied about, don't deal in lies,
Or being hated, don't give way to hating,
And yet don't look too good, nor talk too wise:

If you can dream—and not make dreams your master;
If you can think—and not make thoughts your aim;
If you can meet with Triumph and Disaster
And treat those two impostors just the same;
If you can bear to hear the truth you've spoken
Twisted by knaves to make a trap for fools,
Or watch the things you gave your life to, broken,
And stoop and build 'em up with worn-out tools:

If you can make one heap of all your winnings
And risk it on one turn of pitch-and-toss,
And lose, and start again at your beginnings
And never breathe a word about your loss;
If you can force your heart and nerve and sinew
To serve your turn long after they are gone,
And so hold on when there is nothing in you
Except the Will which says to them: 'Hold on!'

If you can talk with crowds and keep your virtue,
Or walk with Kings—nor lose the common touch,
If neither foes nor loving friends can hurt you,
If all men count with you, but none too much;
If you can fill the unforgiving minute
With sixty seconds' worth of distance run,
Yours is the Earth and everything that's in it,
And—which is more—you'll be a Man, my son!

Secret # 3

Keep Your Head On Straight

IF YOU CAN KEEP YOUR HEAD WHEN ALL ABOUT you are losing theirs ... Kipling's "IF" gives us a powerful beginning to the discussion of this most vital principle of keeping your head on straight, foundational to everything else. It's hard work. You don't "get it together" once and for all. It's a perpetual, in the moment assignment. Having your head on straight is a state of being, a well-adjusted approach to matters of life; a descriptive term for a person whose thoughts are grounded and their life well balanced. In Kipling's poem, "If," he talks about a mental balance that allows one to interact and react to the world at a level of spiritual and mental maturity and polished dignity; that amid the dramatic ebb and flow of life, you remain focused, staying on the high road which sets you apart from others. Keeping your head on straight is a system of self-governance and self-control by the best use of the resources and understanding available, inclusive of life lessons, wisdom passed down, and challenges that unfold along the way. Keeping your head on straight is a delicate balance, a collaborative effort between the mind, the spirit, and the body; managing expectations placed on you by others, meeting the demands of life (family, work), voices clamoring about this and that and everything in between, and still stay grounded.

> "Before a person can accomplish anything of an enduring nature in the world, she must first of all acquire some measure of success in the management of her own mind. If a person cannot govern the forces within herself, she cannot hold a firm hand upon the outer activities that form her visible life.[o]"

Keeping your head on straight is a perpetual "in the moment assignment."

Distractions are everywhere, luring you from your purpose. Keeping your head on straight is keeping your eye on the ball, staying focused and avoiding distractions. It's being down-to-earth relative to self-perception and how you perceive others. It means to think clearly and make good decisions that will have future benefit.[p] It means being realistic about your vision for yourself and how to get there. Having your head on straight is being aware of your strengths, limitations, and what's expedient.[q] Keeping your head on straight isn't an easy, you can do it.

EGO

(Everybody's Got One)

There can be no substantive discussion about keeping your head on straight without giving attention to the understanding of the role of the ego. The ego is somewhat

[o] The Mastery of Destiny, James Allen

[p] Galatians 6:7

[q] I Corinthians 6:12

misunderstood so it gets a bad rap. The definition of the ego changed from the original Freudian thought to the common understanding that it's the measure of what a person thinks of him/herself. A person who thinks highly of their self is said to have a "big ego;" this thing inside that gets out of control, grows into a big monster that causes everyone to hate you. Wrong! It isn't about size, big ego, little ego, no ego. It's about a healthy vs. an unhealthy ego. Don't skip this section.

Per the psychoanalytic theory of Sigmund Freud, there are three parts to the personality, the Id, Superego, and Ego defined as follows:

- **Id**: The instinctual, biological part of self. The id wants what it wants; whatever feels good at the time; no consideration for reality or consequences. Its sole motivation is instant gratification or the "pleasure principle[r]."
- **Superego**: The social part of your personality; your conscience.
- **The Ego**: The conscious decision making component. The ego prevents us from acting irrationally on the desires created by the id. It tries to balance the idealistic standards of the Superego and has the complex task of dealing with the realities of the external world.

The id, superego, and ego work together in creating a behavior. The id creates the demands; the ego adds the needs of reality with the superego adding morality to the action which is taken. Our behavior is determined by the interaction of these three components.

For this discussion, the ego will be the focus of attention because the ego is the component responsible for keeping your

---

[r] The Pleasure Principle is the desire for immediate gratification vs. the deferral of gratification. It drives one to seek pleasure and to avoid pain

head on straight. The ego interacts with the other components in this way: It's like software that tells the other components how to work, allowing you to interact with the world in a proper and acceptable manner. Freud made the analogy of the id being a horse while the ego is the rider. The ego is 'like a man on horseback, who has to hold in check the superior strength of the horse.' (Freud, 1923, p.15). If the ego is healthy, the rest of the personality will stay balanced.

The Healthy Ego (THE)

The healthy ego (THE) is controlled by the "Reality Principle.[s]" The reality principle causes the ego to consider the pros and cons of a desire before deciding to act on it. The ego doesn't try to stop these desires, but tries to achieve them in realistic and acceptable ways. A healthy ego is an ego under control. When you have an urge to do something that you know is inappropriate, the healthy ego (THE) is what prevents you from acting on these urges and offers alternative choices.

When you make decisions, set personal boundaries, maintain self-esteem, take care of yourself, feel good about who you are, and you stand by your values, these are signs of a healthy ego. When you can look at others and not use them as a yardstick for measuring yourself, your ego is healthy. When you can look at another's accomplishments and success without malicious envy or jealousy, but be genuinely happy for them then your ego is healthy. When the ego is functioning as designed, it operates beneath the radar. That, however, doesn't happen

[s] The Reality Principle leads us to delay gratification and behave in ways that satisfies the id's desires in realistic and socially appropriate ways. It weighs the costs and benefits of an action before deciding to act upon or abandon an impulse.

naturally. Like the physical body, the ego needs proper attention to stay healthy. Will power to try to think right isn't enough. To keep your ego in a healthy state, make these low cost premiums an intentional part of your spiritual healthcare discipline:

1. **Prayer**: "Dear Lord, keep my ego under Holy Spirit control today" (or in this situation; or in this moment)
2. **The Word of God**: Short daily devotionals are great
3. **Fasting**: Disciplines, strengthens, cleanses
4. **Giving**: Look for opportunities to give. Giving causes you to think outside of yourself. It causes you to consider the needs of others and positions you to be part of God's solution in the lives of others or a purpose he wants to bring to pass.

The Unhealthy Ego

EGW

Ego Gone Wild

When the ego becomes unhealthy it ceases to function beneath the radar, steps onto center stage and so the drama begins. An unhealthy ego is an Ego Gone Wild (EGW); an ego that's succumbed to the attack of negative influences and temptations resulting in a condition which is easily identifiable in others but virtually unrecognizable in one's self. You've heard terms like, ego mania, delusions of grandeur, cockiness, arrogance, … It's the impetus behind a myriad of things that threaten the health of the ego with peer pressure heading the list. Peer pressure isn't just a childhood phenomenon. It follows us right to the grave, but by different names; self-serving competitiveness ("Keeping up with the Joneses." jealousy, and malicious envy. Will power alone isn't enough. An EGW makes you look like a fool and you're completely unaware of it.

The Egometer

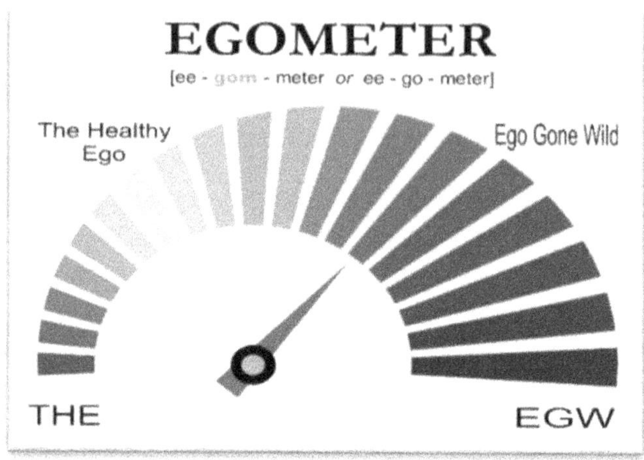

Figure 1 Egometer: A fictional mental meter that measures the "in the moment" health of your ego

Eight Symptoms of The EGW Virus

1. All roads lead to you
2. Whosever has an ear, must hear me
3. You've got to be right all the time
4. You think you're doing it all by yourself
5. Being defensive
6. Interrupting / Not Listening
7. Always able to justify yourself
8. Fault Finder

1. **All roads lead to you**

- You love the sound of your own voice.
- Little to no eye contact during conversation
- You don't listen. You're listening to yourself planning what you're going to say next.
- Somehow the focus always turns back to you.

2. **Whosoever has an ear must hear**

- You assume everyone wants to hear your story, what you're doing or planning to do.
- Ask yourself: Did anyone ask me for details? Is it necessary that I share this? What am I getting out of this? Why am I so insistent?"
- Stop! Check the needle on your Egometer.

3. **You've got to be right all the time**

- You never back down
- You're never wrong
- Backing down doesn't mean you've changed your opinion or admitting you're wrong.
- You shove your opinion into someone else's brain. You can't control what other people think. They may be wrong but so what! BTW, you may be wrong.

4. **You think you're doing it all yourself**

- You're never doing it all. Your EGW will make you think that you're the only one pulling the wagon. The truth is, there's a support team around you, visible or invisible. No matter how insignificant you think their contribution, they're part of the team that got you where you are.
- Acknowledge others. If you think no one did anything for you, check the needle on your Egometer.

5. **Being defensive**

- What are you defending? Is your ego terrified and fragile? Considering another view wouldn't kill you. It might make you smarter. Try it. Instead of your normal knee jerk opposition, you'd be surprised how often giving honest consideration to things that used to upset you now seems interesting or helpful.
- Withholding a reaction doesn't mean you're agreeing, it just means you're secure enough in yourself to give things a second thought.

6. **Interrupting / Not listening**

- You don't always have to say what you think.

LOL!!!
Listen
Observe
Learn

- LOL! Listen. Observe. Learn. Listening is powerful. It cultivates allegiance. It affirms others. People will love you if you listen to them. What do you have better to do? God has brought each person into your life for a reason. If you listen long enough, you'll discover their purpose in your life.

7. **Always able to justify yourself**

- You dig yourself deeper into a hole with weak, "makes no sense" rationale. Acknowledge the wrong and be done with it. It isn't that important. Laugh at yourself and others will be drawn to you and justify for you.

8. **Fault Finder**

- You find fault in everyone. Everyone sins and falls short of your glory. Nobody likes a know it all because nobody knows it all.
- **Stop it.**

EGW Virus Quick Check-Up				
	Symptoms	**Y**	**N**	**Treatment**
1	All roads lead to me			Consider the heavens, the work of God's fingers the moon and the stars,[t]
2	Whosoever has an ear must hear me			In humility consider others more important than yourselves.[u]
3	I must be right all the time			A wise person will hear and increase in learning, a person of understanding will acquire wise counsel[v]
4	I think I'm doing it all w/o help			There's a hidden army of help around you. Open your eyes.[w]
5	I'm defensive			Stop it. Just stop it.
6	I interrupt. I don't listen.			**LOL! Listen Observe Learn.** A fool takes no pleasure in understanding, but only in expressing his opinion[x]
7	I justify myself even when it makes no sense			Give instruction to a wise man and he will be still wiser, teach a righteous man and he will increase his learning.[y]
8	I'm a fault finder			Stop it!

[t] Psalm 8:3, 4
[u] Philippians 2:3b
[v] Proverbs 1:5
[w] 2 Kings 6:17
[x] Proverbs 18:2
[y] Proverbs 9:9

Your Destiny Zone

To find your niche in life, that elusive thing that makes your heart sing; that thing you were born to do; that thing that when you hear the phrase "*do you*," you know what the "*do*" is, is priceless. It isn't always that you don't know what your "*do*" is as much as you don't know how to get there. You know you have more inside of you. You know your thoughts and ideas are beyond the box you live in. You may have a good job, but your job doesn't do it. The people around you are nice but they can't scratch your itch. We may know what the "*do*" is but lack the confidence or know-how to get on the road and "*do you*."

On the other hand, if you're uncertain, then to find your "*do*" seems like such a mysterious pursuit. Everyone has that "*do*" place inside, that no matter whatever else we do, unless it's your "*do*" thing, there's frustration and no satisfaction. There may be a measure of success in other pursuits but there remains a longing for the peace you know is there in your "*do*" space. Whether it's singing on stage, mixing chemicals in a lab, writing fiction or piloting aircrafts, there's a voice we hear in our spirit and an unction inside that wants to get us to the place we were created to be. There's a peace that defies understanding waiting for you there even if the rest of your world is crazy.

Think of it like a zone. There's a zone designed for every gift, talent and calling. When you're in your zone, you're in your destiny space, your unique God space, your Destiny Zone. That sounds exciting, doesn't it? It is. Imagine doing what you love to do. Being the man or woman God has created you to be and being in his perfect will. Imagine being appreciated for what you do. It fits. You feel great about it. No jealousy or competition because this thing you're doing is you! If you feel agitated, unfulfilled, frustrated with just about everything, consider this question. Are you in your Destiny Zone? Don't feel bad if your answer is "No." For countless people, their answer is "No." Here's why. Life happens. You're a kid, then suddenly and without warning you wake up an adult – with a job; kids; responsibilities, and bills; not to mention your own personal issues and demons with which you wrestle daily. The pace of life can be relentless and there's no time to think about how to *"do you."* This is where all the clichés make sense: Life is short. Time flies...... You take care of what's in front of you and in the back of your mind you say, "Someday, I'll ..." You go to sleep one night at 35 and wake up 60. It happens like that for so many people but guess what? Awfully Awesome people start where they are and keep it moving. Late? Maybe. Too late? Never.

Here's a dream buster. You cannot be anything you want to be. Let's deal with this dream buster right up front so that you can walk in victory, live in your Destiny Zone and be on the right road to your God designed purpose. The motivational speakers will tell you, you can be anything you want to be. No, you can't. People tell children they can be anything they want to be. No, they can't. The "can't" has nothing to do with race, or socio-economic location. While the motive for saying that to children is completely honorable, it isn't true. It isn't true for them and it isn't true for you. Wait! Don't get mad. Stay with me. Keep reading.

Everything begins with God. Greatness begins with God. Awesome begins with God. Your ultimate everything; purpose, success and empowerment don't begin with the wonderful, positive affirmations we feed ourselves daily, though they're good and provide encouragement. Everything begins with God. We are God's creation, fashioned by God's own hand for God's purpose. Everything begins with God. Genesis begins with the words, "In the beginning, God ..."[z] He went on to create the world with everything in it and everything with its specific purpose. Then God created this amazing creature called human and gave it purpose; purpose in its relationship with the planet and purpose for the individual being. Look to God first.[aa]

---

[z] Genesis 1

[aa] Matthew 6:33

Understand this. God put his awesome in you. Your potential isn't human potential. The origin of potential is divine. Your potential originated in the mind of God, therefore, there's divine power to make potential a human reality. We are created in the image of God. Rise above that myopic view of visual image. Release yourself from that picture of God someone somewhere out there conjured up and put in the coffee table Bible. The finite mind can't imagine an unimaginable God. God is total and complete, powerful, perfect, awesome in every way. God made us in his image, then he breathed his breath into us. He didn't pump air into our lungs, he breathed his own breath, divine breath into us. The greater than awesome God, creator of every universe, breathed his breath into us. There can ONLY be greatness in you. So, no, you can't be anything you want to be. You can be anything God destined you to be and that's far greater than anything you or I could ever imagine. If you get your willfulness into God's perfect will, then the desires of his heart will be the desires of your heart.[bb] Can you see how the statement changes from "You can be anything you want to be" to "You can be anything God wants you to be?"

To bring God in the mix can be a bit frightening. It's challenging enough to have a dream, to believe in yourself and have enough confidence that you can accomplish it regardless of any obstacles. That's great but awfully awesome people, the best and the brightest know that even when their awesome meter shoots through the roof, they can't do without God. The appreciate the good days when they're feeling strong and unstoppable; but they're wise enough to know there are hills and valleys, ebbs, and flows; times when obstacles don't move just because you believe in yourself. Discouragement and doubt await you on the journey but keep on going. Affirmations have limitations. Acknowledge God who is without limits.[cc] You need to know the Word that has supernatural power. If God

---

bb Psalm 37:4

cc Proverbs 3:5, 6

called you to it, it's his strength that will cause you to succeed.[dd] Recognizing where the dream originated gives you the confidence that failure is not an option with God so it isn't an option for you.[ee]

Stay in Your Lane

It's tempting to jump from one lane to another, especially if you don't have your head on straight or your focus shifts with the scenery. Some people are unaware that they do it. They're like leaves in the wind, all over the place trying to do what someone else is doing, following the latest trend, going with the latest good idea. A lane jumper is a person having no skill beyond the expertise they've conjured up in their own mind and eager to instruct; like the chef trying to tell the plumber how to fix the pipe. Have you been struggling in a place you shouldn't be? Maybe you're out of your lane. Beware! An EGW can jam the signals in your spiritual GPS and cause you to shift lanes. You can be in the wrong lane for miles.

Get in your lane and stay there. That's where your blessing is. It's in your lane. It's on the path that God put you. It's in the gift that God gave you. Stay in your lane. Your lane is your destiny zone. Your destiny zone can be an elusive place if your pursuits are misdirected and your motives incorrect. In other words, you're fashioned[ff], fitted, and called for one journey but you're pursuing another for reasons not grounded in God's purpose. We move in the direction of our focus. You see something you want to be, or someone you want to be. That can be a good thing as long as admiration remains admiration and doesn't morph into a pursuit to claim. Often wrong pursuits are chased in ignorance. To pursue a destiny because you desire the

---

[dd] Philippians 4:13
[ee] Philippians 1:6
[ff] Psalm 139:14

recognition and favor that comes with it is like getting excited sifting fool's gold. It looks like the real thing but it has no value. Think about it. Life will sift you like wheat when you're out of your destiny zone. Here's what it looks like:

- You're trying to be the leader but you don't have the skills for it, nor the vision
- You sing solos when you're perfect for backup
- You're a gifted staff person but you usurp authority
- Pursuing a profession that brings the recognition and respect you desire but you're not gifted for it

You may as well start with your head on straight. Give your ego a check-up so that it functions properly and keeps you in the right lane. Rather than trying to change the dynamics, your time and energy will be far better spent keeping yourself grounded and doing what you've been called to do regardless of public perception. To that end, three concepts come to mind, Sobriety, Humility, and Readiness.

On Sobriety

The word sobriety initially suggests the state of being free and in control of one's self, no longer under the self-destructive influence of external stimuli; specifically, drug or alcohol free. Free of addiction, no longer dependent upon or hooked on any psychoactive drug, psychopharmaceutic, or psychotropic chemical substance that changes brain function resulting in alterations in perception, mood, or consciousness. Under the influence of a chemical substance, regardless of its legality, the effects are the same; blurred vision, impaired judgement, your sense of reason skewed. You can't be trusted and you can't trust yourself.

You can also be under the influence of the wrong person(s), involved in unhealthy relationships, entangled in unfavorable associations, even ideologies that impair your mental health in the same way as substance abuse. Under the influence, to a greater or lesser degree, is a state of not being fully in control of what you think, your sense of reasoning, or choices you make, vulnerable to the strength of the external influence.

Paul broadens the scope of the conversation even further as he warns of another influence that threatens to compromise mental sobriety. You. He says, think with a sober mind; use sober judgement and don't think more of yourself than you ought to think.

Imagine that! Paul links sobriety with having a balanced perception of yourself when he says not to think more highly of yourself than you ought to think. Ought is the word that sticks out. Clearly there is the suggestion to think positively of yourself, but the word "ought" suggests there's a boundary or line between positive self-thought and being unbalanced under the influence of conceit. You can love yourself so much that you get high on yourself, believe your own press, get swept away in the cries of the crowd, "Hosanna, Hosanna," becoming unable to receive wise counsel. Don't underestimate the detriment that can be.

Gird up the loins of your mind.

Get a grip on yourself!

A very well known, highly respected prelate said in a televised, "You don't correct me. I'm not to be corrected. We can talk about it but you don't correct me. I'm not a child." That's dangerously close, if not over the borderline of "ought." Who is anyone to say they are not to be corrected? Everyone needs correction from time to time. Not a child? There is childlikeness within everyone, perhaps more than is recognized, that pushes or sets in motion less than perfect choices. You don't get to decide from where or from whom your correction comes. Keep check on your ego-meter. It's God's prerogative to orchestrate correction. It's our "ought" to accept it. It's certainly important to acknowledge and appreciate your gifts from the Holy Spirit, but equally important is balance and the proper perspective.

It's true, God has a plan for your life and it's good. Peter says "Gird up the loins of your mind …" In other words, get a grip on yourself. You're a vessel God created and gifted for his purpose. It isn't about who you are, it's about who God is. It's what you do and how you carry yourself as you live and walk in the life God designed for you. The responsibilities inherent in your life are many but one of the most important is that you're always aware of the wonder of your creation. You represent someone greater than yourself, and a purpose grander than your own. You're an integral part of a strategic plan that began in eternity past, transcends the now, and extends to eternity future. People are looking at you, and looking up to you; and when they look, they need to see a well-balanced, *ego under Holy Ghost control* person. They need to see someone who knows Jesus more than just on a first name basis.

On Humility

Humility is one of those almost nebulous concepts that despite what a dictionary says, it's difficult to precisely define and certainly challenging to describe. It isn't something you can see, although some interpret physical expressions and appearances as humility. Some synonyms are modesty and meekness; each of which may manifest itself in different ways in differing scenarios. Humility isn't tangible or visual. It's something experienced from another person as you interrelate. It's something you see in a person as they interact with the world and situations around them. It's genuine and real; doesn't come and go nor can it be turned on and off. Humility is a state of mental being informed by one's perception of themselves in juxtaposition to their perception of God; a perception of self in relationship with God revealed situationally. In other words, it would be impossible for a person having a realistic understanding of the awesomeness of God in relationship to themselves, to have an inflated view of themselves, or an EGW.[gg]

Humility behaves with a quiet, powerful strength. It's said, "Knowledge is proud because it knows so much, wisdom is humbled because it knows so little." Wisdom can speak loud in a heart that is humble. Humility calms the annoyance of deadlines because it understands time in eternity; God's time. It isn't driven by competition because it rests in the fact that "what God has for me is for me." Humility trumps jealousy because it understands the concept of running your own race. It prevails against the temptation to envy another's success because it understands how to be grateful for the blessings of others. Humility stills the frustration of delayed satisfaction because it understands the rewards for waiting.

Some are born with a personality that lends itself to a more humble spirit than perhaps others. In others, it may have been developed early in life through teaching. Yet others, for whom humility isn't second nature, it takes a little work. In fairness to those for whom humility is a struggle, consider this. On a whole, the culture of the western world, a capitalistic society, places little value on anything that can't be parlayed into the bottom line, consequently humility isn't necessarily seen as a useful character trait. So, give yourself a bit of a break as you struggle to develop a strength in your character that gets little endorsement or affirmation in the social milieu to which you're accustomed. Self-assess your level of humility. Slow down, pause now and then. Ease your foot up from the gas pedal of your determination, ambitions, and motivations; shift into park on a regular basis. Put "the Will of God" in your divine

---

gg EGW Ego Gone Wild. See "Ego Gone Wild," pg. 10

navigation system. Discern the mind of God on your forward movement.

Humility is looking Godward with self-surrender and sincere desire for God's Will not only in what you're doing but in how you navigate in and through relationships. James and Peter both agree that God gives grace to the humble[hh]. We have only a notion of the incomprehensible value of Grace so if God gives his Grace for humility, then he must place a high premium on humility. It's completely natural as well as a fundamental value in our competitive society to want to do better, and aspire to be the best.

Your better and your best aren't defined by comparison to others

It's incredibly important that you understand this point. Of course, you don't want to rest even for a moment in mediocrity, however, your better and your best aren't defined by comparison, therefore competition holds no true value in the God's sphere. God defines success. God defines greatness. Humility advises, "You're not better than anyone or worse than anyone else. Keep the door open for knowledge and truth to find a place to live in your heart. Then just be your-self. Be your best self.

On Readiness

The meal is ready to eat when the food is on the table. The cake is ready when the oven timer sounds. The baby is ready to be born when the contractions begin. Every call, every new position, every God breathed idea has a gestation period, a learning curve, a process to readiness. It takes time and some

---

hh I Peter 5:5; James 4:6

things just can't be rushed. The wisdom is to know when you're ready.

When you have a dream to do something, a vision for what something can be, or discern a calling, that's just the beginning. That's God just getting your attention, stirring up a desire inside. It isn't time to take off running just yet. That's the time for you to get ready for what God has planned. The desire may be strong and evident to everyone around you, but recognize there's preparation time and wisdom that needs to be imparted. The beginning is the get ready time.

As with most things, you can't see much beyond the now. The realities unfold as you travel your journey. The beginning is the time to prepare for the life, the vision or profession you're being called into. You need time to prepare and cultivate the mind necessary for the destiny you're being called into; and to develop the strength and wisdom that will make you equal to the task laid out before you. You may have been exposed to a profession or skill all of your life, well acquainted with others who have gone before you, have lots of friends in whatever the network may be; though there are common sites in the landscape, the journey for everyone is different. Your ministry, your business, your artistic expression will not be the same as any you've seen. God doesn't need replicas. He's looking for authenticity. He wants those who are able to embrace who he has made them to be and willing to cultivate their thinking to be able to connect with those who need what you have to give.

Cultivate the mind necessary for the destiny into which you're called

When you're called to something, no matter what it is, medicine, ministry, education, entertainment, it isn't for you alone. If God created the desire for it in you and gave you the grace for it, then you will be fulfilled by it; but understand everything created in you is a channel through which God wants to manifest himself to others. That means that with all of your talent, and all of your giftedness, God anoints you as a vessel to serve, encourage, educate, heal, bring deliverance and hope. One of the things Paul speaks of is gifts and how they differ according to the grace and proportion of faith given to us.[ii] It's personal so that we can't do it like someone else. He makes a point about waiting. As exciting and prepared as you feel you may be, it's important to wait. Timing is everything. Timing can mean the different between success and failure. Timing can mean the difference between mediocrity and excellence.

David was anointed to be king of Israel but he had to wait about 15 years from the time he was first anointed by Samuel to the time he became king over Judah. It was another seven years before David was anointed king over all of Israel. That means David waited over 20 years of his life before becoming king over all of Israel. David didn't quit his job as a shepherd and run to the royal apparel store to buy his robe and crown. He remained faithful in his position as shepherd and serving as King Saul's armor bearer and private musician; serving the king he would ultimately replace. This isn't to suggest you'll be waiting over 20 years to see the beginning or fulfillment of your destiny. It is to say that even after you are sure about where you're going you may serve in different capacities before you ever step into the place of your vision. You may be asked to perform menial tasks, things well below your level of skill, giftedness, and preparation, but these are opportunities; opportunities to grow in areas that you've not identified. Opportunities to cultivate, perhaps, the level of humility you need to be trusted in high places. It's your time of "becoming." Beginnings may be less than what you imagined, less exciting, less fulfilling, but don't be discouraged. Before birth there is gestation. Your birthday is coming.

[ii] Romans 12:6-7a

Redeem the Time

In the context of our thoughts in this book, "redeeming the time" means more than making the most of the hours of a day, or making yourself busy while waiting for the manifestation of a promise, a dream or vision. Much counsel is given on the value of waiting. Left without purpose, time consumed with waiting, or waiting being the highest purpose of the time, renders time as merely the empty space measured by the ticking of the clock, an hour, sixty times sixty empty seconds; the day, twenty-four fleeting hours; or the calendar, the month, 30/31 hollow days; the year 365 ordinary days; blank. empty, fleeting, commonplace. It isn't the clock or calendar that measures time, but the deeds with which we fill the time, the feelings and thoughts we give and receive within the moments, a space or spaces to which a definite work belongs.

> Think of time as singular. a season which holds opportunity and purpose

The Apostle Paul uses time in the singular; not times but "the time,[ii]" a season as though there were one duty to be accomplished in that period. Life, within the larger narrative of eternity, is the season for learning to know God, for becoming the full measure of what he created us to be.

Think of life as a whole, an aggregate of consecutive moments, opportunities, a season of your destiny; periods having significance and mission, broken up into smaller portions providing opportunity for a special work.

What would that be? What is that duty? What am I here for? What is the purpose for the whole sweep of my days and

---

[ii] Ephesians 5:16

why to me were they given? Surely not to take my orders from circumstances. Surely not to have a "wait and see what happens" approach to life. Redeem the time. Hmmm. Redeem is a verb, an action word. Redeem is the clear idea of exchange or trade. So what am I exchanging or trading? Time? Can I do that?

Follow the thought that time is opportunity. If time/opportunity is to be truly our own, then something must be given in exchange for it. Paul is saying, you must buy the opportunity; give something in exchange for the opportunity that time places within our reach. What, then will you turn the opportunity into, and how is that done? It's done by sacrifice, by exchanging or giving away the lesser for the greater. Abandon that which serves a lower purpose in exchange for that which serves a higher purpose, a God purpose, a destiny purpose. More simply stated, if in the moment, what you're doing or thinking doesn't serve your God moment, a higher purpose or your destiny, release it. Abandon it. Surrender it to the Holy Spirit. That's what it is to be surrendered to a higher purpose. That's what Paul means by redeeming the time. If we leave God out of our intentional thoughts, seeking his presence in the moment, then we will surely miss God's teaching moment, the wisdom, the necessary principle, the higher purpose of the now. The God time, the divine opportunity will be missed. But, if while we live out our day seeking a greater purpose in that which we do, then we've given away the lesser purpose for the higher purpose, hence, redeeming the time.

	Head Check	Yes ✓	No ✓
1.	**On Sobriety** Do you know Jesus more than on a first name basis?		
2.	**On Humility** I understand, appreciate, and honor the gifts of others, and how I need them to be my best.		
3.	**On Readiness** I'm in ongoing training: seminars, webinars, seminary, online courses?		
4.	Does your focus flow with the scenery; shifting with the best idea of the moment?		
5.	Do you know what's in your "do" space?		
6.	I can name at least three people whom I know personally, whose lives I admire, and I can explain why?		
7.	I can step aside and give someone else an opportunity if I know I'm not ready for it myself.		
8.	I know the principle of "God's timing" and I can handle the wait without bitterness.		

Prayerfully Ponder

1. What does it mean to be down-to-earth about self-perception and how you see others?

2. What does it mean to be realistic about your vision for yourself and how to get there?

3. What are the priorities in your life now and how do they fit in or relate to your destiny?

NOTES

And we being exceedingly tossed with a tempest, the next day they lightened the ship; And the third day we cast out with our own hands the tackling of the ship.

Acts 27:18, 19

Secret # 4

Travel Light

UNPACK YOUR BAGGAGE & TRAVEL LIGHT. In the early years of my corporate career I traveled quite a lot. I enjoyed every part of it, my work, the flights, seeing new places, meeting new people in various positions in my profession. It was work but each like a mini vacation. I enjoyed every part of it except one, the luggage. I'd invested in beautiful luggage. Packing wasn't the problem; even that was enjoyable. But, in those days, there was no curbside baggage check, moving sidewalks, or indoor shuttles. You checked your bags at the flight gate. Therein was the nightmare; getting my luggage through the airport to the flight gate. My only hope was that there might be a motorized passenger cars available; but even those were in short supply and not at every airport. Occasionally someone would feel sorry for me and help me with my luggage but not often.

In an airport one afternoon, I noticed others moving quickly, effortlessly, sitting comfortably at the little snack tables waiting for their flights, while I sat at the gate guarding my luggage, taking up more than my fair share of space. One of my colleagues said, "Your luggage is beautiful but why do you bring so much? You don't need to bring your whole life with you." What an awakening. I honestly thought I needed all of it. I'd become so accustomed to the burdensome luggage that I accepted it as just an unpleasant part of the trips. Believing everything was needed, I never gave a single thought to lightening my load until questioned about it. One seasoned in the position was also a seasoned traveler who knew exactly what they needed for the journey, taking only what was necessary.

FIGURE 2 THE ROOKIE TRAVELER

Inexperienced, rookie travelers take more than they need, costing them extra baggage fees at the airport or schlepping heavy bags through train stations. Onlookers shake their heads at the overburdened traveler. Others may lend a hand. Still others may want to help but are struggling to deal with their own baggage.

Well, I finally got it. I learned two things. (1) Travel came with the position and how I traveled reflected my level of professional maturity as it did the way I handled life at that stage. Don't get stuck at that stage. (2) I had no room for new things I may have wanted to bring home from the trip. God always has new things for us.[kk] Make room for the new. Travel light.

Jesus understood the advantage of traveling light. In neither of the four Gospel accounts or stories about him, regardless of how vivid the imagery, is there ever mention of Jesus carrying luggage. He covered a lot of miles on foot, but never a mention of luggage. Even in the movies he had nothing more than the clothes on his back. When he sent his disciples out on assignment telling them to take nothing with them,[ll] he was asking them to do what he'd always done, travel light. Without tangible things to keep up with, worry about where to store, getting mugged on the road or robbed when they laid things aside to minister, they would be unencumbered,

---

kk Isaiah 43:19

ll Matthew 10:9-10; Mark 6:8; Luke 9:3

unrestrained, and free to focus on their mission. That makes perfect sense if you think about it. They could get what they needed when they got where they were going. The less they took, the less the stress and more the time and mental energy available for their assignments. Surely the disciples had the normal life issues that may have caused distraction but that wasn't the subject of Jesus' concern. If there weren't the potential hindrance to completing their assignments because of tangible things, then Jesus wouldn't have bothered to tell them to take nothing with them.

Note to Self:

It's okay to have things, if the things don't have you.

The accumulation of things is the norm in a consumerist culture. Too often the volume or expense of one's possession is the measure of their self-worth, judged by themselves and others. Cars, clothes, jewelry, real estate, art, antiques, … God's world is beautiful and he's put things here to be enjoyed. Things for which to be grateful. It's okay to have things if the things don't have you. What does that mean, if the things don't have you? It means, the more you desire, the more you acquire; the more you acquire the more is required. Tangible things can almost seem to take on life. They require attention, maintenance, replacement, repair, etc. They come with a cost; bills, mortgages, insurance, warrantees, credit cards, memberships, etc. Things must be paid for. This isn't an admonition to live a life of monasticism unless that's your thing.

The more desired, the more acquired.

The more acquired, the more required.

One thing awfully awesome people are conscious of is good financial management; debt control. Debt very subtly becomes your master. Debt will own you and your time. When you have debt and you bow beneath the weight of it, your thoughts are consumed with how to get from under it. Another way to put it is, you can be a slave to debt. Debt puts limitations on your freedom. Once enslaved to debt, your choices are no longer your own. You can't spend your money or give because you've already spent it, so whatever you get in the future must pay for the past. Too much debt means too much worry. Debt demands overtime, hence, less time for the things of God and the things God has for you to do. Debt is a heavy weight. Beloved, travel light.

Note to Self:

Just because you can buy it doesn't mean you can afford it.
- C.D. Lawrence

Check Your Bags

Imagine at birth being given one empty piece of luggage, a carry-on piece, in which to keep your life experiences. See the instructions on the tag. The purpose of this piece of luggage is to enable you to conveniently keep with you the experiences you need, and lessons learned. The piece of luggage is marked MEMORIES. Although everything goes in, good and bad, you don't need to keep everything. Some experiences are by choice, so be careful what you pack. The more you pack, the more there is to unpack. Things get in your bag in several ways. You put them there (avoidable mistakes; self-inflicted wounds); other things are dumped on you by others via their meanness, cruel words, insecurities, ignorance, whatever.[mm] Other times it's just things that come with living; unemployment, illness, death of a loved one, bad breaks, etc. In the final analysis,

[mm] See Secret # 7 "Watch Your Mouth"

it doesn't matter what caused the pain. Pain is pain. Whatever happened, happened. It cannot unhappen. The question is, did you unpack your bags from the experience?

Life is a common experience.[nn] To move through life with good strength and agility, you must do maintenance by looking through your luggage, keeping what's good and unpacking what isn't. Good things happen and we find joy and praise God for the good things. Bad things happen, some quite devastating. Good or bad, experiences leave behind residue, and that's what you're looking for, the residue. You cannot undo an experience but you can clean up the residue. Tsunamis, earthquakes, terrorist attacks happen. The tragic mess left in the wake can be cleaned up so well that nothing is left but the memory. You can't undo the tsunamis that came in your life. You didn't see it coming; you didn't ask for it; you didn't deserve it, but you can clean up the mess and live with the memory. **Live in the now**. **Embrace the now.** It's hard to comprehend that all things work together for good,[oo] but they do. All things aren't good but they work together for good. At the very least, the "good" is what you've learned from the experience. Ask yourself the question, "What has this experience done **to me**, or **for me**? What residue has it left behind in my life? The residue left behind is what you decide to keep or discard. Keep what is valuable, praise worthy, life giving, instructive. The rest is garbage. Do what you do with garbage. Throw it away.

Note to Self:

Some experiences are by choice. Be careful what you pack. The more you pack, the more there is to unpack.

If you don't unpack, let go and stop hoarding painful memories, insults, the dregs in the life experience, they'll take up

[nn] 1 Corinthians 10:13

[oo] Romans 8:28

increasingly more space. Instead of discarding the bad stuff you'll add extra luggage to accommodate the load. Now you've officially got baggage! Baggage to drag around everywhere you go, heavy with the vestiges of life's experiences. By the way, people can see your baggage.

Look at this poor soul on the next page. Maybe the "Do Not Remove" tag fell off his one piece of carry-on luggage and he never knew to check, unpack and dump. Maybe he thinks that's how life is supposed to be. He continued to add more pieces to hold the memories, until he finally needed a wagon to carry it all. In his wagon, there's no room for joy, hope, or praise for life. Maybe unkind, uncomplimentary words were hurled at him at a young age that shattered his self-esteem making it difficult, if not impossible, to believe in himself. Maybe there was no one there to tell him what he heard was untrue. No one to tell him he was fearfully and wonderfully made.[pp] Maybe he was raised in an environment of criticism, someone asking "Why can't you be like your cousin or the boy down the street?" leaving him insecure. Maybe he got a bad break in a business deal with a friend, and now he's angry. Maybe he's late middle age and he thinks his dreams will never happen and he's bitter and depressed. There's a cliché that says, "Time heals all wounds." Not so. Wounds, hurts, habits, memories, broken dreams, disappointments, bad decisions, regrets, … become baggage, intangible baggage.

Didn't see it coming
Didn't ask for it
Didn't deserve it
BUT!!!
You can clean up the mess & live with the memory

Where's his inner circle? Either he doesn't have one or the inner circle he has doesn't have the right people in it. If his inner circle was effective they'd say, "We'll help you to throw

---

[pp] Psalm 139:14

that stuff off your wagon." There are a lot of good people pulling a wagon like this. If this is you, don't skip Secret #6, "Choose Your Inner Circle Wisely."

Figure 3 Don't let this be you!

Life, Incorporated

Imagine life as a company and you've been hired. Welcome to the company, Life, Inc., you're now on the clock. Here's the deal. You can go about doing everything as right as is humanly possible and suddenly life will throw you a curve ball or deck you with a sucker punch. You'll be assaulted by life. You won't cause it. You won't see it coming. You won't deserve it. You'll get sick on the job but no time to nurse your wounds. The company keeps moving even when you slow down or stop. Heal on the go, so to speak.

Life, Inc. offers no time off and no sick pay. Life, Inc. offers no workman's compensation or time off for healing. You show up when you're sick and heal while on the job. It's hard but that's Life, Inc. You know the importance of priorities and responsibilities and you want to handle your job in mature and honorable ways. Great! but understand Life, Inc. shows no partiality for good behavior. It's equal opportunity experience. It rains on the just as well as the unjust.[99] Life, Inc. does not

[99] Matthew 5:45

have a department called mercy. You need mercy? For that you'll have to seek God.

You say to yourself, "I'll be okay." And for the most part you may be okay because you're awesome and you can function, so you shake yourself, close your bag, ignore it, feel strong and move on (so you hope or so you may think)? Unresolved issues follow you and affect your life in terms of relationships, decisions, perspectives, in ways that you're unaware of until after the fact. In life unless you intentionally inspect your bag regularly, keep only what you need, unpack, and dump the rest, it will stay in your bag. You can fake traveling light but people will see your baggage and smell your garbage. You may need help unpacking. Nothing wrong with that. You may feel alone but you aren't.[rr] That's one reason the 6th Secret about your inner circle and their value in your life is so important. Your inner circle isn't just a group of friends who conveniently hang out together. Your inner circle has purpose; to help you get to your purpose. Say it with me again. Life happens. Everyone accumulates baggage but you don't need to keep it.

Lighten Your Load Before the Storm

In Acts 27, Paul was a prisoner being taken by sea to Rome, Italy, to appear before the court of Caesar. During the trip a fierce nor'easter arose threatening the lives of everyone on board and destruction of the ship. The men did two things to lighten the load to save the ship. First, they threw cargo overboard. Second, they threw the ship's equipment overboard. Everything they threw overboard was considered important enough to carry onboard, but when the storm hit and their lives were threatened, they threw those things overboard.

[rr] Refer to The 6th Secret, "Choose Your Inner Circle Wisely"

What's happened in your past matters: Circumstances of birth, mean things people said to you as a child, horrific childhood traumas, divorce, multiple marriages, job loss, loss of dreams, all kinds of life experiences. Your past matters. Say it with me, *"The things that have happened in my life matter."* Our experiences shape us; shape our perceptions of things around usand our outlook for the future.

No one should ever deny your life experience or belittle the impact all of it has had on who you are today. The totality of your life matters. Now here comes the "but." But that isn't the end of the story. Your life story is being written as you breathe each breath. The end of your story has yet to be written. Whatever happened, happened. Mourn while you move. Respect the past and the experiences, appreciate the moments. Here comes another "But." But, you can't live there and you cannot bring it back. You can never regain what you have lost, only lose what you have gained. Don't wait until there's a storm in your life to lighten your load. Travel light.

Note to Self:

Storms will come, most often without warning

Be mindful of what you're taking onboard life's journey

Never hesitate to get rid of stuff you *think* too important and can't live without

You can never regain what you have lost, only lose what you have gained.

Call to Action

Give God something to work with. You need to have a plan. Information is in abundant supply, online everywhere from social networks to webinars, books to seminars. Good stuff. Great stuff. Motivational speakers, preachers, self-help books and good friends, all pass on invaluable information, awesome life information. BUT! Beloved, only taking in information can sometimes just be a way to scratch an itch. Information can be like comfort food. It makes you feel good to know this and that. You can feed on it but if you do nothing with it, it has no more value than reading a book about healthy nutrition while you lay on the sofa eating a two-foot-long hoagie, fries, a diet soda and a big piece of triple chocolate cake sitting there for dessert. You must do something with what you know if you want to release the awesome in you.

Information can be like comfort food

Make a plan. It doesn't have to be perfect. You can tweak it and change it along the way, but you've got to start somewhere. Changing a bad habit (whatever it is) takes time, but the countdown clock doesn't begin ticking until you take the first step in your plan. When you put your plan in motion, then the God of the universe gets in that plan with you. He'll work out things that you can't figure out. He'll make crooked places straight that you're unaware are crooked.

The faith walk begins with
the first step, no matter how small

- CL Lawrence

Prayerfully Ponder

Name ten things and/or people you know you need to remove from your carry along bag. Check Yes or No if you have a plan.	**Yes** ✓	**No** ✓
1		
2		
3		
4		
5		
6		
7		
8		
9		
10		

What's in Your Carry Along Bag?

1. Do you have unresolved issues from your past following you? Circle each that applies or write your own.

- Are you angry with anyone?
- Did someone betray you in a relationship or business?
- Do you have an issue of un-forgiveness?
- Guilt. Did you wrong someone?
-

2. Are you wrestling with insecurities? Yes _____ No _____

What's the plan?

____

____

____

3. Is there anyone in your inner circle and/or outer circle who shouldn't be there? Yes ______ No _____

What's the plan?

____

____

____

4. Are there any habits in your baggage that shouldn't be there?

Yes _____ No _____

What's the plan?

____

____

____

NOTES

Nurture your mind with great thoughts, for you will never go any higher than you think.

— Benjamin Disrael

Secret # 5

Always Have A Teachable Spirit

PRICELESS. PERHAPS THE MOST IMPORTANT secret of all. For many people a teachable spirit doesn't come naturally, but with discipline, however, it can be learned. It's totally unnecessary if you walk the avenue of "get over;" or the boulevard of mediocrity. It is, however, a non-negotiable characteristic necessary to walk the path of excellence. It's benefit to you, it's worth to those with and for whom you work and serve, is beyond measure. We don't come ready-made, ready to hit the ground running. We come into the world or into situations with gifts and skills that need to be developed, honed, and perfected. You must be ready for the process, the preparation for perfection. Preparation seems long and boring. You see where you want to go but the road looks longer and more tedious than we think necessary. Remember this, necessity is the tablet upon which your testimony is written; never revealing itself until the end.

Extraordinary and awesome are lights seeking to be revealed, yet, without a teachable spirit, remain under the bushel of potential.

In the 1950s, 60s, and 70s, mostly guys would sing on the corners and in the subways of major cities; beautiful voices, perfect harmony, yet they never made it past the street corners. Other talented individuals, even less talented, from the same neighborhoods made it big, got recording contracts, appeared in movies, etc. Was it luck? Was it an unseen genie who granted their wish, or a coincidence lottery they won? When you listen to their stories, there's a common thread throughout the ones who "made it." They listened to the advice of credible people. They listened to wisdom. They followed directions. They were open to instruction even when they didn't want it.

The greatest waste in the world is the difference between what we are and what we can become.
- Ben Herbster

Without a teachable spirit, you won't know what you need to know, never fulfill your God-given abilities and potential, or enjoy your God-given gifts and the fruits they bring. Of course, there are many other dynamics that direct one's course to their destiny. It would take volumes to give space in a book to them all. But there is one dynamic that demands attention, a teachable spirit.

> *"Reprove not a scorner, lest he hate thee: rebuke a wise man, and he will love thee. Give instruction to a wise man, and he will be yet wiser: teach a just man, and he will increase in learning"*[ss]

There are exceptionally gifted people; business people, public servants, musicians, singers, writers, preachers, artists,

---

[ss] Proverbs 9:8-9

dancers, … whose gifts cannot be denied but talent would be so much greater if they'd accept instruction and direction from others who have *been there/done that*, instead, preferring to "do what comes naturally." A teachable spirit is something that manifests its presence or its absence.

A teachable spirit is relevant to those in areas other than the arts. What about the person who wakes up suddenly 60 and realizes their future holds no financial security because they didn't take investment advice in their youth? What about those who can't balance a check book; who have credit scores equal to their body weight because they refuse to invest the time in understanding how money works. What about the one whose brilliance is obvious to everyone in the company but their career plateaus because they refuse mentorship?

A person with a teachable spirit can be taught, and is receptive to wise counsel without being defensive or feeling belittled. They may be asked to do something that others would feel is beneath them, and they may even feel is beneath their skill set or position (a menial task on the job, run an errand, get the coffee, be involved in the youth department when that isn't your passion, …). The person with the teachable spirit doesn't define themselves by what they're asked to do. They define themselves by how they see themselves and where they're going. They see the not so lofty steps along the way as opportunities to learn and take from the experience that which will give them what they need for the future. They apply what they learn.[tt]

A person with a teachable spirit doesn't see the now as anything more than the purposeful experience or necessary pathway to an expected end. One with a teachable spirit can be trusted in high places, trusted to represent the king among kings, so to speak. They can be trusted to take to the experience what they've been taught and bring back what they've learned. God

[tt] "The true value of being teachable comes when we take something that we learn and apply it." John C. Maxwell

can pour himself into a teachable spirit and know the result will reflect himself.

We're here on purpose and for a purpose. God has a purpose for your life. He didn't just get a good idea and then decide to call or choose you to make it happen. He predestined you before the foundation of the world. He saw and fashioned you in your mother's womb with a destiny and a purpose. The Holy Spirit imparted in you the gifts you'd need to fulfill God's purpose in you. He designs experiences for your growth. We're fine with the good ones, but it's the not so good experiences we protest. The truth is, we grow in the difficult times, in the belly of the great fish, in the valleys and on the backside of the desert. In those times, we find difficulty with all things working together for our good and for those called according to God's purpose.[uu]

A person with a teachable spirit sees the now as a purposeful experience; a necessary pathway to a greater purpose.

God orchestrates our intersections, who we meet and the point in time in which we meet. Sending people in your life to groom you, help you to interpret your experiences, and give you the wisdom you need to go forward in excellence. God brings others who may have a different view or approach to something because diversity adds dimensions to our own realization of truth. Seldom can we perceive a situation in its entirety. Others can offer the benefit of new approaches that will expand our understanding and comprehension. In other words, God gives us everything we need in the spirit realm and the earthly realm to get us where he wants us to go.[vv] The one with the teachable spirit gets it. A teachable spirit is the most important principle of excellence and exceptionalism in life,

---

[uu] Romans 8:28

[vv] Philippians 4:19; 2 Peter 1:3

relationships, parenting, career mobility, ministry, … If you've voluntarily plateaued, reaching a place where you can/will no longer learn anything, then you've stepped out of the progressive arena of life, and assumed the posture of a non-entity, unnecessary, not useful, a non-contributory.

12 Dead Giveaways of a Teachable Spirit

1. Humility (See Secret # 3)
2. Awareness of limitations, knowledge, & abilities
3. Willingness to admit limitation, inability, and ignorance to those who can teach and help
4. Willingness to ask for help, instruction, guidance, and advice (before, not after disaster strikes)
5. Hungers for wisdom
6. Willing to learn from anyone
7. Willingness to receive wise counsel; open to suggestions and new ideas – even when they don't understand or agree
8. Seeks and nurtures collegiality & values committed mentoring relationship
9. Views correction as a path to the greater possibilities; willing to try new things; moving beyond their comfort zone
10. Takes responsibility
11. Sees failure as not a reason to give up. Will seek help and try again until they get it right.
12. Views adversity as an opportunity to try something better.

Unteachable

An unteachable spirit isn't veiled, but boldly out there for the world to see and hear. They're heard because they always have something to say. They have the answer before the question mark. They have the solution before understanding the scenario. There're some dead giveaways of a person with an **un**teachable spirit, which you can see on the following page. The #1 dead giveaway is, they're a "know it all.[ww]" The "know it all," knows it all, and no one likes a "know it all." There's nothing you can teach them because they know it all. They have all the answers, the know-how, with no relevant experience, leaving others to wonder from what knowledge base they draw. They're almost always struggling, continually trying to get past mediocrity, competing where there's no competition, abounding with explanations and excuses. Their receptors are clogged with "my way" residue and the dregs of self-aggrandizement. There's no openness to be enriched by others.

Any leader would prefer a less gifted person with a teachable spirit than a highly-gifted person who can't take direction and correction. Better to be less gifted with a teachable spirit then to be a highly gifted "know it all." An unteachable spirit will cause you to miss God's best.

The Bible says the steps of a good person are ordered by the Lord ...[xx] Thy word is a lamp unto my feet and a light unto my path ...[yy] God does not give us the road map or the blueprint of our destiny. It's a faith walk, very often, one step at a time, a process through which learning takes place. The one with the teachable spirit will learn. For the "know it all," there's nothing to learn because, well, they know it all.

[ww] Erwin G. Hall, "We can't learn anything new until we can admit that we don't already know everything."

[xx] Psalm 37:23

[yy] Psalm 119:105

Ten Dead Giveaways of an Unteachable Spirit

1. A "Know-it-all." Never been there; done that; no T-shirt
2. Believes their own press
3. Loud and wrong
4. Doesn't take notes, read books, or learn anything unless required
5. Doesn't ask questions
6. Doesn't accept responsibility for failures; blames others
7. Doesn't look for or accept personal guidance
8. Doesn't listen, but talks, talks, talks about themselves, especially when with someone from whom they can learn
9. Doesn't take criticism or correction without resentment or retaliation
10. Doesn't read, listen to, or learn anything that challenges existing presuppositions, practices, and prejudices

	Is Your Spirit Teachable?	Yes ✓	No ✓
1.	Do you have a willingness to receive wise counsel w/o feeling defensive?		
2.	Are you aware of your limitations and abilities?		
3.	Do you welcome the consideration of alternative thoughts and differing points of view (different from yours?		
4.	Are you receptive to direction from more experienced others?		
5.	Do you view correction as a path to the greater possibilities?		
6.	Do you feel appreciative when someone tries to give you wisdom?		
7.	Do you feel comfortable when someone questions the direction in which you're going (decision)?		
8.	When someone points out an inconsistency, do you shift into explain mode?		
9.	Are you proactive when it comes to training, self-development, and getting the information you need?		
10.	Do you implement and act on the ideas and principles you receive?		

Learn as though you were to live forever. - Mahatma Gandhi

NOTES

The Eagle Who *Thought* He Was a Chicken

A baby eagle became orphaned when something happened to his parents. He glided down to the ground from his nest but was not yet able to fly. A man picked him up, took him to a farmer and said, "this is a special kind of barnyard chicken that will grow up big." The farmer said, "don't look like no barnyard chicken to me." "oh yes, it is. You will be glad to own it." The farmer took the baby eagle and placed it with his chickens.

The baby eagle learned to imitate the chickens. He could scratch the ground for grubs and worms too. He grew up thinking he was a chicken.

Then one day an eagle flew over the barnyard. The eagle looked up and wondered, "what kind of animal is that? How graceful, powerful, and free it is." Then he asked another chicken, "what is that?" The chicken replied, "Oh, that is an eagle. But don't worry yourself about that. You will never be able to fly like that."

The eagle went back to scratching the ground. He continued to behave like the chicken he thought he was.

Finally, he died, never knowing the grand life that could have been his.

Secret # 6

Choose Your Inner Circle Wisely

BIRDS OF A FEATHER FLOCK TOGETHER. WHEN you look around and take inventory of the birds in your flock, you might be tempted to dispute that truism, but before you do, check your feathers. There's something about those in your circle, some commonality, whether obvious or subtle, that attracts them to you and you to them. Take a moment to digest that. It happens without any effort at all; people stay in their comfort zone, around people with whom they're familiar and have much in common. Billionaires Warren Buffett and Bill Gates are friends; Oprah Winfrey and Gayle King are friends. No disrespect or offense intended, but when did you last have a casual lunch with the mayor of your city or chat about the state of the country with the host of Meet the Press? Who else in your circle was there? People gravitate toward others who are likeminded, in same or similar professions, socio-economic location, share similar philosophies, etc.

It's a great thing to have family and friends in your circle. There's a feeling of security with the familiar and there's a level of nurture that only the familiar can give. Nevertheless, receive this caution. Your comfort zone is fertile ground for the roots of mediocrity to grow deep and strong. Your comfort zone is just that, the place where you're comfortable. You know the rhythm of the environment, what's expected of you and what you can expect from others. No one pushes you to go higher because average becomes the norm and people become complacent in the usual. No one rocks the boat; no one challenges you to take a half step above the ordinary because when you do, that raises the bar for everyone. Many people are just fine operating at the level of mediocrity. Perhaps not you. Maybe you have more in your reservoir but in your comfort zone more isn't needed. It's a rut and you need to get out of it.

That's what this sixth secret is about, your world, your circle, more specifically, your inner circle. Time passes without notice. When you live in the complacency of ordinariness your spirit becomes lethargic, curiosity finds no energy and creativity finds no egress. The new things God has for you to bring to the world becomes someone else's assignment.

If you confine yourself to a small, homogeneous environment, you'll restrict your growth to the level of your self-imposed limitations and that of those around you. Jesus didn't do that. Think about it. Think about the different places he went and different people he encountered and his interaction with them. Just that alone speaks volumes about the model of openness he set forth. A small world, a myopic world view, only yields a recycling of the same thoughts, ideas, opinions, and interpretations. Complacency allows you to regurgitate what you've heard unedited. You need to expand your circle to include others who can stimulate your growth. Surround yourself with people of wisdom, experience, and spiritual insight; and

> A small world view recycles the same thoughts, ideas, opinions, interpretations, and expectations.

then ask God to allow some of it to rub off on you. Build relationships with creative thinkers. Others who, regardless of age, are excited about the journey of life, new things to discover, different ideas to explore. Expand your circle to enrich your life, stimulate personal, intellectual, creative, professional, and spiritual growth, not just for yourself but for the people God will place in your sphere of influence.

How do you do that? Be intentional about having conversations with people who may think a little differently, who aren't in your church or family. Talk to people not in the same school, neighborhood, or workplace. The internet and social network are great tools if you use them properly. Check out news shows you wouldn't ordinarily listen to, people from around the world. Just check out what God is doing beyond your own little world. If you want to be in a bigger space in this amazingly diverse and beautiful world, you can. The right people will come into your sphere. Be ready to receive them

The Tabula Rasa (blank slate) theory of human development, credited to English philosopher, John Locke and Swiss philosopher Jean-Jacques Rousseau, was first documented in the late 17th and early 18th centuries. The theory says that humans are born with no knowledge, an empty mind, completely free of any predisposition or vulnerabilities, and that knowledge from experience and the effects of the environment shape and define who a person becomes. Therefore, a person has no identity until after birth.

We now know, of course, that isn't true. Mothers feel the temperament of the baby while they're still in the womb especially in the last trimester. Babies tend to have a sleep pattern while still in the womb. We can see little personalities in babies almost immediately after birth. Some are calm, others are fussy. Some respond with a smile and baby babble only days after birth. Others seem to ignore any efforts to get a response from them. The Bible teaches that we were known by God before the foundation of the world, that he breathed himself into us, so we were not born blank slates. However, the part of the theory that's of interest is the idea that external influences have such strong power in shaping and molding lives. Through associations you form your world view, you get to know yourself better. As you broaden the boundaries of your world you see more of yourself and you see more of God. That can be frightening to a person who needs to see God as familiar and predictable, his ways logically explainable, in a nice neat little box.

As you broaden the boundaries of your world, you see more of God.

The first step to broadening your sphere of influence is allowing yourself to become comfortable with ambiguity; be okay with being unable to explain everything that has to do with God. Be okay with something or someone God may bring into your world that may seem like an unlikely friend. The person may be of a different race, a different socio-economic level. God is eternal. He cannot be contained. He cannot be fully known. The more you know of him the more there is to know. You cannot drain the well of who God is so ***stretch, stretch, stretch*** yourself to see more. As you see more and allow God to do more in your life, he will bring people into your life you may never have reached out to. He knows a lot of people, he has a bigger network, and he knows who to send to impact your life for an amazing future.

If you have a gnawing, unrest inside, a feeling that says, "There's got to be more to life than this, more to the world than this," then that's the Holy Spirit putting the little eagle's view of the sky in your spirit, telling you that there is more. If you want to go to where there's more, then you need to leave the chickens and develop a network of eagles. A network that transcends where you are now. This isn't to suggest that you cut your family ties or shun your lifelong friends. It simply means you need to do some work in your garden, perhaps transplant some flowers. Enlarge your territory. Open yourself to relationships with people who have big ideas, big dreams, ambitious plans, meaningful purposes; people who generate the energy off which others can feed; energy that invigorates you to achieve your goals. New flowers in your garden don't have to be the same. They don't have to be exactly like you or be in the same profession to be in your inner circle. There is so much to be learned as others share their gifts and the wisdom of their experiences. If you're the smartest one in your circle, then your circle is of very little meaningful benefit. Boring. Just a recycling of the same old conversations and the same old points of view. You'll never grow in that circle and you'll never be happy there. Ask yourself if you have the need to be the smartest one in your group. If your answer is "yes," then getting therapy would be a good idea. Get your head on straight.

What is an Inner Circle?

Let's start with an understanding of your inner circle. Look at the visual illustration on the next page. That's "you" standing in the middle. The circle of people closest to you is your inner circle, your closest group of friends. There may or may not be family members in your inner circle. These are they whom you reach out to first when you want to make certain your new idea makes sense. These are the ones you call when you have a mountain in front of you that needs to be moved. These are the friends whose advice you trust. Your inner circle are the people who are up close and personal, who know your hopes and dreams, your goals, and visions. They know your fears and weaknesses. They want your highest good and they want you to make it. Your inner circle are your champions, your protectors. They celebrate your good and cover your bad.

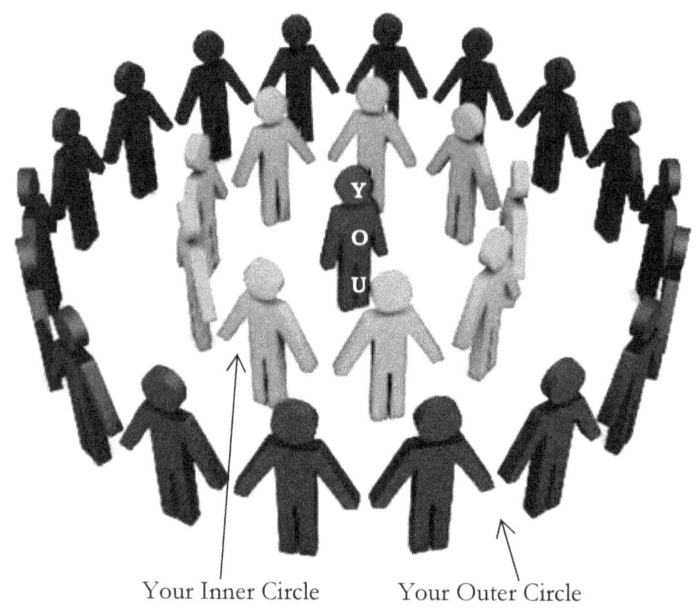

The next circle of people is your outer circle. These may be family, neighbors, or associates. That which differentiates inner circle friends from outer circle friends is the depth of friendship. There are those in your outer circle who you may call "friend," but you can't share your deepest goals and visions. You know they won't understand. Those in your outer circle may want the best for you but they can't help you get there. Perhaps their world view is too small. Perhaps they have limited ability to see. Some people just like things to remain the same.

"Who's Who" in your Inner Circle?

Jim Rohm, personal development expert, said, "We're the combined average of those we spend most of our time with."

Now, that's reveille, your bugle call, your trumpet call, your loud wake-up call. The people you're spending your time with may be nice, sweet people in many ways but they may not be the picture you envision of yourself. You may have to use some photo editing software on the picture of your inner circle. You may need to airbrush someone out or overlay someone in. The important thing to know is, you have the tools to create your picture the way it needs to look for your life goals. No one else can do it for you. No one else can see the God given vision for your life. They can see if you paint the picture for them. But you must see it and own it for yourself first. You will never be invested in what someone else sees or tells you is for you. God gives that to you first. When you own it, then you'll know who to bring into your circle. You'll know who belongs. You'll know the voices that create your harmony.

You may be like the eagle in the story. He was acting like the chickens because there were only chickens in his inner circle. But there was something on the inside that knew he was more than a chicken. Chickens don't fly and they don't want to. You need to be deliberate and strategic in choosing your inner circle friends. If you want to fly, if you believe you can fly, you need to be around people who want to fly; people who've flown, who've seen life from a higher vantage point.

Who's who in your inner circle matters. It's so important that you choose wisely those who comprise that space in your world. You're judged by the company you keep. The people who are consistently around you, in many ways, define the perception of who you are and the heights to which you will go. So, who's who in your inner circle?

How does one get to occupy the coveted position of being a part of your inner circle? Jesus had thousands of followers, but he chose twelve disciples. It wasn't whosoever came along could come along. He carefully chose the twelve which strongly suggests that you give attention to who's in your outer circle as well as your inner circle. Of the twelve there were only three in his inner circle, Peter, James and John. They were the ones with whom he shared his most personal thoughts, plans and ideas. They were the ones with whom he shared intimate moments of prayer, pain and disappointment. What qualified them to be his inner circle? Just because a person is related to you, lives in your neighborhood, or has known you for a long time, doesn't qualify them to be a part of your inner circle. You may love someone dearly but that doesn't qualify them to be a part of your inner circle. It isn't selfish or snobbish to hold the view that what a person brings to your life experience now and potentially, positions them to be considered a candidate for your inner circle. This is your life and you're responsible to take care of it wisely.

You will never rise any higher than the circle around you.

What do they bring? Everyone has baggage. The fact that a person has lived past the womb means they have baggage. If you're inviting someone into the inner circle on your life journey, you need to check their bags; see what experiences they're bringing. They may seem like a good fit, but as much as possible, you want to get a look at their inner circle to see who they're bringing with them. Your friend may have a friend that isn't your friend. Your friend may have associates you don't see. Though they're invisible to you, you may feel their presence and influence channeled through your friend. Influence via association is a fact you cannot control but you can be aware of it as much as possible. Do a baggage check.

Do a baggage check

The people you have around you significantly influence your progress. That which is around you rubs off on you. If you spend time with jealous, critical, unhappy people, you'll soon become the same. You need to be in the right mix. That may require you to prune off relationships that don't add anything to your life. You can't hang around chickens and hope to fly with eagles. In other words, don't spend your time with people who are unmotivated, sloppy and going nowhere; people without goals and dreams. Don't spend your time with people who are undisciplined, who have no focus, for whom mediocrity is the norm. They may have a good heart. They may not be bad people. They just aren't good for you!

There's much written about the personality traits, character, and characteristics that you should look for in candidates for your inner circle. At the top of the list is to have people of strong unshakeable faith and a deeply rooted positive attitude. Invite people who speak positively about things; who have good things to say about others; who see great possibilities. The Bible has much to say about speech and the power of the spoken word. Death and life are in the power of the tongue. You need people who speak life into your life and life into the atmosphere. Words spoken reflect what's in the heart. Positive words are life giving and have the power of encouragement. Listen to their speech; people reveal themselves in their conversations. They tell you exactly who they are

- Do they send out positive energy into the atmosphere?
- Do they send out praise for who God is, what he's done, and what he's capable of?
- Do they have an Ephesians 3:20 confidence?

You need people in your inner circle who know and believe the Word of God and have faith in his promises; people who so exhaust themselves with the positive that they are too tired to be negative. You can always find people who will play "the devil's advocate." You don't need that. The devil doesn't need any more advocates; he has an army of his own. You need people who are likeminded in that they believe in themselves, believe in you, and have big vision and know God is bigger than any circumstance, any obstacle and able to bring to fruition any vision he's placed in your heart.

The Second Ending To The Eagle's Story:

He looked up and flew

with the eagles.

Will you stay on the ground clucking with chickens?
- Or -
Will you look up and spread your powerful wings and
fly with the eagles?

How will your story end?

Prayerfully Ponder

	Vet Your Inner Circle	**Yes** ✓	**No** ✓
1.	Do they inspire you to stretch yourself beyond your comfort zone?		
2.	Do they encourage you to think bigger, try new things, consider new ideas and fresh perspectives?		
3.	Do they challenge you to think outside of the box?		
4.	Do they add value to your life? If yes, how?		
5.	Do they have relationships with champions?		
6.	Do they encourage you to be your best self?		
8.	Do they hold you to the goals you've set for yourself? (Accountability partnership)		
9.	Have you checked their bags?		
10.	How do they speak of people close to them? (Circle one)	+	-

Live as though you were to die tomorrow.

Yes or No answers only get your thinking started
Think deeper:

1. On a separate sheet of paper, list the people in your inner circle, and what they do for a living. Are they moving forward or have they been in the same position for years?

2. What have you done as a result of their encouragement to stretch yourself beyond your comfort zone?

3. What new things or new ideas have been a result of their encouragement?

4. How have they encouraged you to think more broadly? If so, how?

5. How do they add value to your life? How are you better because of them?

6. Who are the encouraging and influential people in their lives?

7. What are their visions and goals for their life?

NOTES

"I learned that you actually have more power when you shut up."

- Andy Warhol

Secret # 7

Watch Your Mouth

WE'VE ALL HEARD THOSE WORDS GROWING up. From the earliest possible moment we teach children words and how to use them; what to say, how to say it and when to say it; good manners, please and thank you. There are those intense moments when we teach them what not to say. We teach them to pray, then tell them "watch what you pray for" or "careful, you might get what you ask for." OK, well isn't that the point, pray for what you want and expect to receive it? We issue the warning without explaining what that means consequentially. In other words, words have power, energy and life. They are spoken in the moment but they have no expiration date.

Words have no expiration date

In 1977, Earth, Wind & Fire's "I'll Write A Song For You," there's a poignant line in the lyrics relevant to this subject, "Sounds never dissipate, they only recreate in another place." You understand and cope with the death of everything, dreams, ideas, initiatives, churches, civilizations, dynasties, political reigns, dinosaurs, pets, and people – BUT – there is no such thing as the death of words. Once spoken, they go out, synergizing with that which we cannot see and have no control, triggering the consequences, good, bad, or otherwise. When something has innate power, we have limited control of its results. That's what the Bible is trying to teach when it speaks of the tongue in 160 times,[zz] (53 times in Psalms and Proverbs alone), the majority of which either warning or illustrating the power of the tongue to bless or curse.

The tongue's power over death and life isn't to say we have the power to say who lives or dies. It does mean, however, that the words we speak have the power to influence and control the quality and direction of our lives, and in many scenarios, the lives of others. Take a moment to digest that reality. If death and life are in the power of the tongue, imagine what power it yields in-between life and death. Could you ever imagine having that much power? Well, guess what! You do. It's a power each of us has. This discussion will cause you to think about how you use it.

Words communicate our thoughts and feelings. A phrase can be spoken in one way and perceived in a myriad of ways. One word can make a difference. Based on the Bible, attention to speech, language, and words, we can never give enough attention or caution. The Bible speaks of life and death, ascribes power over each to the tongue, all in the same short scripture.[aaa] Death? Thou shall not kill, is a moral imperative included as one of the Commandments in the Torah.[bbb] The demand to not kill is in the context of unlawful killing resulting in bloodguilt. The Hebrew Bible has many prohibitions against unlawful killing, but also has strict laws for lawful killing in the context of war, capital punishment, and self-defense. What's being discussed within the frame of this thought isn't about

---

[zz] KJV

[aaa] Proverbs 18:21

[bbb] Exodus 20:13 and Deuteronomy 5:17

physically drawing blood, but about life and death; the power of words to give life to the living or death before dying.[ccc] Words have that much power.

The tongue like a sharp knife. kills without drawing blood.

God *spoke* the world into existence. Words can be used to command an army to kill a multitude of people, destroy cities, and execute innocent people. They can also be used to hurt people around us, those we don't know, and even people we love. Words communicate thoughts, ideas, emotions. Great people with the skillful and deliberate use of words throughout the centuries have caused minds to change, moved hearts to transform, given birth to new movements that pushed the pendulum of society toward new social and religious paradigms. To name only a few:

Jesus
J.F. Kennedy, Jr.
M.L. King, Jr.
Nelson Mandela
Winston Churchill
Malcom X
Abraham Lincoln
William Folkner
Mahatma Gandhi
Demosthenes
Malala Yousafzai
Barack Obama
Michelle Obama
Margaret Thatcher
William Wilberforce
Maya Angelou

Speech writers, marketing experts, con-men (and women), cult leaders, savvy sales people, femme fatales, gigolos and Casanovas know the power of words to persuade. Billions of dollars are moved every minute of the day because of the power of words. If that is true in the larger narrative of history and the world around us, how much more is it true in the personal arena of life. Look at the power of words:

[ccc] Proverbs 18:21

THE POWER OF WORDS Words can either		
Encourage yourself and others toward excellence		Push yourself and others into a downward spiral of hopelessness
Make situations better		Make situations worse
Build up faith in self and others	or	Build discouragement
Build hope		Cause gloom
Draw people to you		Push people away
Be used for good		Be used for evil
Heal		Hurt

Respect the Power

The Bible says you shall have whatsoever you say.[ddd] Words can act "either/or" with equal efficacy because – say it with me – *Words have power.* The effect of words isn't coincidental. You choose words and how you use them for the result you have in mind. That's why the cliché, "Think before you speak." Think of what will happen if you say it this way or should it be said another way, use different words, or perhaps not say it at all. You can say something but you have no control over how it's perceived. You do, however, have control over what you say and how you say it BEFORE you say it. How you speak to and about something or someone matters. How you speak to and of yourself matters. Watch Your Mouth!

[ddd] Mark 11:23

Break the Habit of Negative Speech. Start Now!

If someone talked to you the way you talk to yourself, would you call them "friend" or foe? It's uncomfortable to say positive and affirming things about yourself for fear of sounding haughty or prideful; so, it's easier to make self-deprecating comments. "I'm so stupid." "I'm never going to make it." I don't have what it takes." The problem is you begin to believe your self-published negative press, even if only published in your mind, and kill your own self-esteem. **Stop it! Just stop it!** It isn't always the things that people say about you that hurt you, it's the things you say about yourself that can be of equal or greater harm. Negativity calls into the atmosphere a cloud of doom, oppression, and depression. When there's negative and critical talk going on, there's no joy or encouragement in the atmosphere. You don't feel joy when you walk away from a conversation full of gossip, complaining, or judgmental talk, not even in conversation with yourself.

Break the habit of negative speech. Start now!

Negative talk is habitual; a very easy habit to fall into. There are always negative, dissatisfied people around so negative conversation is plentiful. It's a habit that brings no honor or praise to God, therefore it's a habit that needs to be broken. Start now! Breaking any habit takes time and diligence. Just like with losing weight; you don't just stop eating the bad stuff. You replace the wrong foods with the right foods. Even if you lose weight initially, it's just a temporary experience unless you continue to practice good eating habits until it becomes a way of life. Negative talk is a habit and just like any other habit, it can be broken. It isn't easy, but you can do it. You must do it. To replace habitual behavior, you must replace it with something else and diligently practice the replacement behavior. Let's be specific. You must replace negative talk with positive talk. It's more than just repeating positive motivational declarations. They're great and quite useful, but to reach the level of change that's necessary, the complete make-over you really want, you must go deeper. You must first realize that negativity does not become you. You are the manifestation of divine imagination so negativity anywhere in your sphere is a contradiction of who you are. The transformation you're looking for begins within your heart and mind.

You are the manifestation of divine imagination

The first step in the retraining process is teaching yourself a new way to think. That begins with remembering you're fearfully and wonderfully made.[eee] That means you're the right height, the right weight, the right race, the right complexion; born in the right country, at the right time in history, to the right parents, with the gifts, talents, and qualifications … Everything you are is right for the journey and the destiny God designed for your life. You may have preferences different from that which you naturally possess (hair color, length, texture, body type, eye color) and you may choose to make cosmetic alterations. That's your choice, but it doesn't make you better than God's original "you," nor does God like you any better. So, go ahead, feel free to fool around with the outside, it's the heart that is the locus of change.

Confession

The Bible puts a very high premium on confession, what the mouth speaks. Both Paul and John speak about how the

[eee] Psalm 139:14

confessions of the mouth leads to salvation, forgiveness and cleansing of unrighteousness.[fff] Since our verbalizations come from the heart, such confessions can only come from a heart that has been cleansed and created anew. Otherwise a confession would be empty words.

"What we confess with our lips dominates our inner being.[ggg]" You tell yourself what to believe about yourself. That's why it's so important that your speech is always positive and up building. What you say repeatedly, you come to believe. Never say things like, "I'm so stupid." or "I'm an idiot." Why would you say that about yourself? Why even take a chance that you might, somehow, in the recesses of your being, possibly believe it. Say words that encourage your own soul that empower you; give hope and determination.

You shall have whatsoever you say.[hhh] That is to say, you drive the course of your actions with your speech. The Bible isn't talking about "hocus pocus," *say it, wait a minute, then you'll have it by sundown.* The principle applies either in prayer or in speaking, you direct the course of your actions; actions into which God intervenes (or not). I'm going to finish school on time. That will make you manage your time for your studies, develop effective study habits so that you can accomplish that goal. I'm going to have a new vehicle next year. That confession will make you develop and honor a realistic budget, improve your credit score and drive off the lot with that new car the following year. I'm going to have the promotion to the next level in my job in 18 months. That will make you diligent in your work, more creative in your thinking so that you stand out. My income is going to increase because I want to give more than just 10%, I want to help a single parent family. I want to donate regularly to a domestic violence shelter. If you're faithful in your

---

[fff] Romans 10:9, 10; 1 John 1:9
[ggg] F.F. Bosworth
[hhh] Mark 11:23

giving, God will give you ideas that will put more resources in your pocket because the desire of your heart express your advocacy for the desires of his heart. If there's power in words, then let the power work on your behalf. If it's in your heart and you speak it, then you will direct your actions in the direction of your speech. Those are awesome declarations of faith that lead to actions, and God can put blessings into actions of faith.

A Matter of The Heart

The fact that what's in the heart is revealed in one's speech[iii] is simply reason enough to make a thinking person want to keep their mouth shut. A shower every day, maybe even twice a day, deodorant, tooth paste and mouth wash, all designed to cleanse the body so that it won't be offensive. But, who thinks of cleansing the heart so that their words won't be offensive. In the old days if you were caught saying bad words, the teacher or your mom would wash your mouth out with soap. YUCK! While profanity, the use of those four-letter words is unbecoming and beneath the dignity of people of a holy nation,[iii] this secret is concerned with something far more damaging, far more lethal than "bad words." It's concerned with the power in the choice and use of words. When we read the word "tongue" we know the Bible is referring to words. Words can be used in ways that heal encourage and motivate others to fulfill their greatest potential, and bring leaders of nations to find common ground. Without the use of a single cuss word, words can be used to cause doubt and despair, start wars, and destroy the bonds that hold relationships together. There are no cleaning products, from

> Be quick to listen and slow to speak.
>
> James 1:19

---

iii Luke 6:45

iii I Peter 2:9

mouthwash to industrial strength grease solvents able to cleanse mean spirited/dirty words or their effects once they're spoken. The best oral hygiene is powerless to sanitize words as they come out of the mouth because words come from the heart.

Let your speech be always with grace, seasoned with salt, that ye may know how ye ought to answer every person.

Colossians 4:6

Have you checked what's in your heart lately, or ever? Please, don't be offended by the question. Think of the heart as a reservoir or storehouse. As a reservoir, are you pouring in fresh water daily, keeping the water moving. Is your heart a channel where living waters flow? John says, *"He who believes in Me, as the Scripture has said, out of his heart will flow rivers of living water."*[kkk] As a storehouse, are you storing the Word daily, fresh food that will nourish, strengthen, and give hope, or are you storing stinky garbage, like undisciplined judgmental thought processes, anger, painful memories. Take a look at your Ego Meter;[lll] check yourself for the EGW virus.[mmm] Daily spiritual cleansing, cleansing of the heart is as important as daily physical cleansing. *For of the abundance of the heart the mouth speaks.*

This is so critically important. The fact is, you can't smell your own breath. Other people know your breath is offensive but you don't. You figure it out from their reactions. Once you do, you take steps to address it, right? Take time to notice how people react to your communication. The old people used to say, "You can't smell yourself right away. By the time you smell yourself, you've been stinking for three hours." Truth or old wise saying, who knows? Unarguably, you can become accustomed to your own body odor. Likewise, you may not be

[kkk] John 7:38
[lll] Ego Meter, See 3rd Secret, Keep Your Head On Straight
[mmm] EGW: Ego Gone Wild, See 3rd Secret, Keep Your Head On Straight

Sidebar: On Forgiveness

Forgiveness must be included in any discussion of offense. In such matters, the Bible clearly states the imperative to forgive. (Matt. 6:13; Lk. 11:4).

As the wounded party, we must always forgive. We're scripturally bound to do so. Difficult? Yes. Unfair? Perhaps, but forgiveness is a small price to pay for freedom from anger and its destructive consequences.

As the offender, while God has forgiven, grace grants the expectation and hope of forgiveness from the offended party. Grace doesn't, however, grant the freedom to carelessly or premeditatedly offend nor does it afford diplomatic immunity.

Don't freestyle with a lethal tongue, then play the "grace card" for forgiveness.

Watch Your Mouth!

able to hear your own voice. Take time to look around. You might find your words have left a trail of wounded and dead bodies on the side of the road behind and around you.

Teaching about the tongue gets a lot of print space in the scripture because God wants us to understand the power you have in speech, the power of words. Between Genesis 1:3-30 (KJV), God talks a lot. Nine times it's written, "God said, …" speaking things into existence. He talked a lot in those 27 verses, using words to bring things into existence, giving directives concerning how each entity was to function. What's so incredible about the power of God's words just in the creation alone is that all remains in operation as spoken from the beginning. In John 1, Jesus is called the Word that was present in the beginning, and now made flesh. The Word was crucified but the Word was also resurrected, and with power. Can you see the association of power and word? Ephesians 4:29 gives a quite vivid description of what words can do, especially insulting slurs and words spoken in anger. Words have meaning and they can be spoken too quickly. They can be like a sword thrust into the heart of the hearers, bringing irreparable harm to the one to whom they're spoken. The Bible says guarding your mouth preserves life but the person who lets whatever comes up come out ruins him/herself.[nnn] Is that you?

Let's take the high road here and assume you're a perfectly sweet and nice person who would never intentionally say anything to hurt anyone, but you have a lethal tongue. It may not be your intention to do damage with your tongue but intention doesn't soften the impact of the rock you throw or lock the trigger. If you shoot someone accidentally, you may be Godly sorry, but they're still shot and wounded. If you repeatedly shoot someone, eventually something inside of them is going to die, emotions, hope, dreams. You can fall on their casket of emotions and lie on their grave of lifeless hope with deep genuine sorrow but they're still dead. Living but dead.

Scars Remain

Wounds heal but scars remain. In anger, horrible, ugly words with a deadly effect may be spoken. With absence of malice, words spoken in jest can wound a tender spirit. The tongue should be kept sheathed until it is routinely under control. Indeed, God has already forgiven you and your victim may have forgiven you for each rock you threw and shot you fired, but, they're still dead. Just as Jesus called Lazarus and others from the dead, and God raised Jesus from the dead, resurrection is certainly possible. Notice, however, resurrection didn't happen to everyone and in each instance, it happened to that person only once. The question is, how many times can you kill someone and expect them to rise again? A rather dramatic way of saying, Watch Your Mouth!

[nnn] Proverbs 13:3

How ironic it is that the very thing upon which verbal communication depends, the thing that has the power to channel living waters and/or death dealing cruelties, is the very thing needed to encourage and build each other up and cultivate relationships. The tongue directs traffic at the intersection of Grace and judgement, condemnation and affirmation, life, and death. As the heart is the reservoir from which the tongue draws its speech, James says, first, "Out of the same mouth proceedeth blessing and cursing. My brethren, these things ought not so to be."[ooo] Then, confidently poses this question: "A spring doesn't send both fresh and bitter water from the same opening, does it?[ppp] David asked God to create in him a clean heart.[qqq] He prayed that God would "Set a watch, O Lord, before my mouth; keep the doors of my lips."[rrr] David understood the power of words; the power to be destructive otherwise he wouldn't have asked the Lord to set or guard his mouth.

The heart is the reservoir from which the tongue draws its speech

Wisdom is the reward you get for a lifetime of listening when you would have preferred to talk.
- Doug Larson

If you can't be silent, you'll have nothing to say.
- Hans Finzel.

Speak only if it improves upon the silence.
- Mahatma Gandhi

ooo James 3:10
ppp James 3:11 (CJV) Complete Jewish Version
qqq Psalm 51:10
rrr Psalm 141:3

The devil's Advocate

Throw this term away. Stop using it. Perhaps with a harmless motive one uses this term with the intention of pushing another to consider the opposite point of view, they say, "I'm playing the devil's advocate. The question is, "Are you playing or is that your regular MO (modus operandi)?

Don't dignify the devil. Why would you even want to identify with the devil? Why would you imagine that you could use the devil for anything remotely good? If he should stop by and thank you for your support, you wouldn't like that.

D D D

Don't

Dignify

the devil

The devil doesn't need any more advocates. He has quite enough. Be an advocate for speech which pushes the conversation forward and in a positive more dignified. direction.

Watch Your Mouth!

Memory Verses

1. Death and life are in the power of the tongue, and those who love it will eat its fruits. Proverbs 18:21

2. Let no corrupting talk come out of your mouths, but only such as is good for building up, as fits the occasion, that it may give grace to those who hear. Ephesians 4:29

3. But what comes out of the mouth proceeds from the heart, and this defiles a person. Matthew 15:18

4. There is one whose rash words are like sword thrusts, but the tongue of the wise brings healing. Proverbs 12:18

5. A word fitly spoken is like apples of gold in a setting of silver. Proverbs 25:11

6. Whoever guards his mouth preserves his life. Proverbs 13:3a

7. A gentle tongue is a tree of life, but perverseness in it breaks the spirit. Proverbs 15:4

8. Let your speech always be gracious, seasoned with salt, so that you may know how you ought to answer each person. Colossians 4:6

9. Pleasant words [are as] a honeycomb, sweet to the soul, and health to the bones. Proverbs 16:24

10. Wherefore comfort yourselves together, and edify one another, even as also ye do. 1 Thessalonians 5:11

Prayerfully Ponder

Speak Life • Speak Healing			
Are the words I'm about to speak		Yes ✓	No ✓
1.	Positive		
2.	Negative		
3.	Encouraging		
4.	Life giving		
5.	Affirming		
6.	Is there a better way to say this?		
7.	Helpful		
8.	Demeaning		
9.	Adding value to the discussion?		
10.	Would I mind them being repeated?		

Prayer: *Lord, let the words of my mouth and the meditation of my heart be acceptable in your sight, O Lord, my rock and my redeemer. (Psalm 19:14); set a guard, O Lord, over my mouth; keep watch over the door of my lips! (Psalm 141:3). Help me each day to bring honor to you with my speech. Amen.*

NOTES

NOTES

If you know the enemy and know yourself, you need not fear the result of a hundred battles.

If you know yourself but not the enemy, for every victory gained you will also suffer a defeat.

If you know neither the enemy nor yourself, you will succumb in every battle.

— Sun Tzu, The Art of War

Secret # 8

Flee Jealousy & Envy

MEET THE INFAMOUS TWIN DEMONS, jealousy and Envy. They travel together, look alike, often behave alike, people confuse them, but make no mistake. They're different. It's well worth your time to know them and clearly recognize the distinct difference between the two because left unleashed these two emotions are very formidable enemies, skillfully stealth in taking down kings and queens, destroying nations and killing hopes and dreams without shedding one drop of blood, although they have been known to be the impetus behind malicious criminal behavior, even murder.

In the fifth chapter of the first letter that bears his name, Peter issues a wake-up call using two strong words, sober and vigilant. To be sober is to be clear minded and free from the influence of anything mind altering. Vigilant is to be watchful and cautious. You need to be sober and vigilant at all times in this life. Use your sanctified imagination and envision twin lions, Envy and Jealousy, stalking you day and night. The surest path to defeat in any adversarial situation is to underestimate your enemy. Don't make that mistake with these two. Envy and jealousy are emotions, deceptively similar but different. In one way, they are even each other's opposite: envy is evoked when someone has something good that you want, jealousy when you have something good that you believe someone else wants to have. Envy involves a longing for what you don't have. For example: If Pastor Wonderful craves a mega church like Bishop Awesome, he's envious of Bishop Awesome. If he's upset about maybe losing his members to Bishop Awesome, he's jealous. Emotions are powerful. With equal dexterity, they can motivate you to greatness with enthusiasm or to destruction with the ease and precision of a lion's powerful swipe.

Both these emotions lie within the flesh to a greater or lesser degree. The frequency and intensity of their appearance is primarily contingent upon individual personality, temperament, the way one looks at the world, and spiritual maturity. Whatever you're called to do, you're subjected to internal struggles, the war between the flesh and the spirit which Paul so thoroughly and eloquently describes.[sss]. It's important to understand from two vantage points and multiple perspectives how envy and jealousy operate. You can be jealous or envious, or the object of someone's jealousy or envy. Both are considered here.

Envy

To feel envious of someone, you need to compare yourself to that person. You can envy someone's intelligence, good looks, social position, or relationship with a person. In each of these cases, you determine that the other person is better off than you, and that you would want that good thing for yourself. Psychologists suggest there are two types of envy: Benign Envy and Malicious Envy.

[sss] Romans 12:14-24

When You Envy Others

(Benign Envy: The Safe Zone)

Benign envy is the kind which raises you up rather than making you want to pull the other person down. It carries a positive connotation, a type of emotional stimulus that moves the person to aspire to be as good in whatever way as the object of their envy. It can be used to express a desire to equal another in achievement or excellence as in emulation or admiration. In this notion, it's used in a complimentary sense without negative implications. If you say, "I envy Michael's ear for music arrangements. He is truly an architect." This is a positive statement, quite complimentary. If you stop there, you're in the safe zone. There is, however, a very fine line separating the Safe Zone from the Danger Zone.

When You Envy Others

(Malicious Envy: The Danger Zone)

We tend to feel malicious envy towards another person if we think their success is undeserved. This is the type that makes us want to strike out at the other person and bring them down a peg or two. Malicious envy also includes the judgment that the other person does not deserve the good thing, so not only do you want to have the object for yourself, you also want the other person to not have it anymore.

Spiritual Gifts, for example, are distributed at the discretion of the Holy Spirit. They are unique to you, customized to your personality, temperament, etc. Your gift is so designed for excellence that if you stir up the gift within you and seek to perfect it, it will operate on the level of excellence for which it was intended. The problem enters in when the system of human evaluation is placed on the spiritual gifts, ascribing a "pyramid of value;" some gifts more valuable than others, therefore, some more desirable than others; or the different administrations of the same gift having differing levels of esteem. Here stalks the lion of malicious envy, a negative emotional influence that ruins a person and his/her mind causing the envious person to blindly want the object of their envy to suffer in some way. They may not want the person to step in front of a bus, but maybe that the sound system die in the middle of their solo; or let them get stuck in traffic or have a flat causing them to miss an important meeting.

Listen to the conversation between Greg and the Holy Spirit as human value enters the picture in the case of Greg and Michael. Notice how Greg focuses on Michael's talent.

Greg: Michael is a genius at arranging all genres of music. I wish I had that gift. I have a decent ear but not like his.

Holy Spirit: *Arranging isn't the gift I've given you. I've given you the gift of writing soundtracks for movies, TV, theater, etc. How will you use what I've given* <u>*you*</u>*?*

Greg: Yeah, but I want to do what Michael does. If I work at it, I can do it just as good, maybe better than Michael.

Holy Spirit: *Yes you can do it, but you'll never do it better. That's not the gift I've given you.*

Greg: Yeah, but I want to do what he does. I know I can do it. Hmmm. In fact, I don't really need Michael in the studio anymore. I can handle what he does.

When the Holy Spirit called Greg's attention to the gift of writing soundtracks, Greg didn't acknowledge his own gift. He recognized that Michael was a genius so the envy wasn't negative or personally against Michael at first. Greg saw something he admired in another person. Nothing wrong with that – but he didn't stop there. He crossed the fine line and stumbled into a downward spiral landing smack into the danger zone. Admiration took a back seat to covetousness, a desire to have what Michael had. Finally, instead of recognizing the gift and talent in himself and devising a plan to develop his gift, his plan was to dismiss Michael and operate in the gift he wanted instead of the gift he was divinely given. Subconsciously, quickly and subtly, envy can become negative and personal causing one to enter the danger zone.

You may honestly and without malice admire a gift, talent, or special ability another person has, a charismatic presentation style, a political wit, a better job, a more supportive family. Admiration is honorable. Just be cautious. Envy can turn into a sneaky foe. Admiration can fall prey to malicious envy with covetousness wherein you no longer admire but you desire. Now you have a problem. If you don't bring that feeling under subjection to the Holy Spirit you'll find yourself consumed with the desire and taking manipulative steps to get what they have, or if you have the power, outright take what they have.

Envy doesn't always start out as admiration and desire to emulate. Sometimes envy starts out bad. You've heard of people, perhaps even known one or two who envied the advantages, possessions, notoriety of a colleague, or friend; things they desired but lacked. They undermined the person in order to take it. That's called "back stabbing." There is no other term for it. Backstabbing.

When Others Envy You

You may find yourself the focus of another person's envy, benign or malicious. Always keep your humility meter fine-tuned through prayerful relationship with God. There are three things you must do when you become aware of envy by a colleague: (1) Keep your head on straight; (2) Commit the matter to prayer; and (3) Keep a safe distance. Take the high road and assume there is no malice intended but you can see how quickly one can go from the safety zone to the danger zone when envy degrades from admiration to covetousness. You have a responsibility to use wisdom to protect yourself. Remember the roaring lion is seeking to devour.[ttt] Your admirer might suddenly get hungry. You've seen others in the danger zone and you don't want to fall victim to that. To be the object of someone's admiration is affirming and feels nice. Everyone needs affirmation from time to time. Just prayerfully remember that the affirmation is for that which God alone has placed in you. It's the God in you that they see.

Jealousy

Jealousy is having the fear that someone is going to take what you have. Jealousy is having the fear and suspicion of losing one's position or situation to someone else. Jealousy has to do with holding on to what you have because you fear that someone else is going to take it away. The operative word is fear. While fear is a vital response to physical and emotional danger, if you didn't feel it, you couldn't protect yourself from legitimate threats, however, fear of loss as defined by jealousy is entirely different. There may or may not be a basis in reality concerning the threat of the loss, but there is certainly a feeling of resentment and generally describes a sort of emotional rivalry between people. When it comes to jealousy, there is no safety zone. When jealousy appears, it takes you in only one direction. Down. Think about it. If you fear that

> Jealousy is the fear that someone is going to take what you have.

[ttt] 1 Peter 5:8; Ezekiel 22:25;

someone can take something, that describes the feeling of inadequacy. They have the power to take. Jealousy begins to talk to you saying, "You have to fight to keep what you have." Both envy and jealousy breed feelings of inadequacy. When you feel inadequate anger sets in and everyone around you becomes actors in your play.

When You're Jealous of Someone

Real or imagined, you perceive someone has the power to take something from you. You become distracted from your work and focused on the fight. That person becomes your rival. Even if it's only in your mind, your perception is your reality and you act accordingly. Follow this short hypothetical scenario:

> There's a young, very gifted person on your staff, or your team. People are excited about her, saying how good she is at the job and what an asset she is, great personality, etc. They're saying you should allow her more responsibilities, give her more visibility. You may not recognize it at first but you feel a little something stirring up on the inside. Jealousy is beginning to take root as it did with Saul toward David. (I Samuel 18)
>
> Your imagination gets the better of you and you begin to imagine the person is trying to undermine you, steal the respect and admiration of the rest of the staff until she steals your job. Little by little you find yourself finding faults in the young staff member. You're becoming less friendly toward her, less encouraging and more critical. When others speak of her you find fault. You begin to cut back on her responsibilities for no reason other than the fact that you have the power to do it, until finally the young staff member transfers or resigns.

The reality is this. What God has for you is for you. No one can take anything away from you that God has given to you. You can give it away by being ungrateful, mediocre, or by succumbing to jealousy, but no one can take it. That doesn't mean they won't try; it just means they won't succeed. Suppose they can sing better, teach better, possess better skills in other areas of leadership. So what! You have what it takes for your divine assignment. If more were required, you would have been given more. Don't waste your precious personal capital of resources on being jealous. "Do you." Be your best "you."

When Someone is Jealous of You

When you're the object of someone's jealousy, you're in a very dangerous position. You're in the crosshair of the "fiery darts of the wicked." Don't try to rationalize it or look for logic. There is none. If their jealousy of you goes unchecked, it will only degrade. It isn't the same as being the object of an admirer's envy (Envy in the Safe Zone). Be very clear about this. Jealousy is a murderer. Jealousy would claim self-defense but that plea would never stand the scrutiny of the Holy Spirit. Jealousy commits premeditated murder; spiritual murder in the 1st degree. The one guilty of murder by jealousy is guilty of the included lesser charges: anger, malicious envy, hatred, meanness, plotting, as well. It's most formidable weapon is the tongue; with the tongue, it can take you out. Jealousy will try to hurt you, demean you, embarrass you, discourage you, exclude you, eliminate you, destroy your reputation, undermine your work. Jealousy will do anything that will take you out of its equation.

Murder by Jealousy

~

Spiritual 1st Degree Murder

A person's jealousy toward you is not your fault. The problem lies within that person. You, however, as the object of another's jealousy, do have a threefold responsibility. (1) Compassion wants you to understand a jealous person isn't a bad person, but they are an insecure person. The seed of their insecurities were planted long before you ever came on the scene. Don't take it too personally. You're just a convenient target. There were others before you and there will be others after you. They would be jealous of almost anyone. Think of how it must feel to have an emotion that rises up within and gets out of hand. Jealousy doesn't travel alone; it's companions are envy, anger, spite, hatred, just to name a few. For a colleague to be jealous of another, it can't be a good feeling. No one enjoys being out of control. Being ruled by any emotion can't be a pleasant experience. In the midnight hour, in those dark quiet moments when no one else is around, even if but for a moment, the jealous person is not proud but rather ashamed of their feelings. That's not to say it's okay. It's just a reminder that compassion has a voice in this matter.

Gird up the loins of your mind.

Get a grip on yourself!

Secondly, your responsibility is to protect yourself and your purpose. Within the context of this concern you can't make someone not be jealous but you can guard yourself if or when you find that you're the object of their jealousy. Of course, you cover the matter in prayer. It's bigger than you are. Jealousy has far too many warrior companions for you to deal with alone. Be smart and keep a safe distance from a jealous person. You can't fix jealousy. You can't love jealousy away, or love someone out of their jealousy. Step back! This demon is for the Holy Ghost alone to handle.

Thirdly, keep watch on your "humility meter." Make sure you aren't doing anything to kindle the flame of jealousy in another person. Watch your mouth to be certain you aren't bragging in any way without realizing it. Be sure your verbal praise and thanksgiving isn't a veneer for bragging. Humility says, "Whatever good is in me, I'm grateful to God for it and for the privilege of using it to God's glory." Paul says it's God who has begun the good work in you and it's God who performs it through you.[uuu] Keep your head on straight.

Finally, this closing thought about jealousy. Jealousy is, above all things, an extreme lack of faith in God. It speaks loudly in one's spirit saying:

- God has given you less than someone else
- Someone else is better
- What God has given is insufficient
- God will allow someone to take what you have.

Jealousy doesn't see the big picture; the purpose God has for bringing people into each other's lives. Jealousy is insecure and selfish, often caught up in one's own self-centered thoughts, thinking only of itself and what it imagines it stands to lose.

fight malicious envy and jealousy with all your might. Know that what God has for you is for you. No one can take away what God has purposed for you.

[uuu] Philippians 1:6

Prayerfully Ponder

1. Are you jealous of someone today? If so, why? Be honest.

____

____

____

____

2. What does a jealous spirit say about one's perception of God?

____

____

____

____

3. Note three scriptures that address the matter of jealousy.

____

____

____

____

ENVY & JEALOUSY	
ENVY **2 Entities** **At least 2 people**	**JEALOUSY** 3 Entities 2+ people & 1 object of desire
You Want Something Someone Else Has	Afraid Someone Is Going To Take What You Have
Doesn't always carry a negative connotation	Always implies a feeling of resentment toward another.
Can be used to show a desire to equal another in achievement or excellence as in emulation. Desire to emulate doesn't have negative connotations.	Always negative
A reaction to lacking something	A reaction to the threat of losing something (position; notoriety)
The emotion when you want a position or notoriety that someone else has	The emotion when you fear you may be replaced in the affection of the people you love
To bear a grudge toward someone due to coveting what that person has or enjoys	Apprehensive or vengeful out of fear of being replaced by someone else.
In a milder sense: the longing for something someone else has without any ill will intended toward that person	It can also mean watchful, or anxiously suspicious.
When one lacks a desired attribute of another person.	When something we already have is threatened by another.

NOTES

Pray for my soul. *More things are wrought by prayer than this world dreams of.*

Wherefore, let thy voice

Rise like a fountain for me night and day.

For what are people better than sheep or goats

That nourish a blind life within the brain,

If, knowing God, they lift not hands of prayer

Both for themselves and those who call them friends?

For so the whole round earth is every way

Bound by gold chains about the feet of God

- Alfred, Lord Tennyson

Secret # 9

Link to the Cloud

& MAKE HEAVEN YOUR HOMEPAGE. CREATE an account (a relationship with Jesus), and Stay Logged In. You need WIFI (Word Inspired Faith Ignited) that powers your connectivity to the Cloud. Mentally Hyperlink positive scriptures. Bookmark every blessing for quick recall when you need them. The Holy Spirit is your data. Without WIFI you have limited data; with WIFI you have access to unlimited data. Choose the plan that's right for you.

WIFI
Word Inspired
Faith Ignited

Prayer is the breath of an awesome life. So fundamental that prayer metaphors are everywhere. The wind tunnel of the Ruach. The flight path of the anointing. The raceway of divine power., the tracks upon which the blessing train runs. Each metaphor, a channel. Consider the latter, the train track for prayer. The power, anointing, insight, spirit sight, boldness you need to be strong in your life comes down on the track of prayer you lay. Imagine every prayer is a railroad tie, bolted down by faith. You lay the tracks that allow the power, healing, and blessings of every kind to get to their destination.

Your track is only as strong as the quality of your railroad ties and the care you take in laying each one. Just as with physical railroad tracks, regular maintenance is required to make sure the train can get to its destination without incidents, interruptions or delays, so it is in the spirit realm with prayer. Tracks of prayer need regular attention to be strong enough to sustain the power that needs to come down the track. The more chaotic the world, the more power needed and the stronger the track needs to be.

Imagine people waiting for the train with the cargo of blessings they need coming down your track. Imagine even yourself waiting. Is there enough track for the train to come down? Is the track in good repair, strong enough such that the powerful train of blessings can come down or is the track weak and the train has to move slowly? People are waiting for the train coming in on your tracks. If your tracks are weak and raggedy, that could cause delays. A disciplined prayer life keeps your tracks in good repair; keeps them well-oiled for smooth locomotion.

A disciplined behavior of any kind, eating, exercise, study, reading, resting, etc. takes time to establish and purposeful action to maintain. Isn't it interesting how easy it is to develop a bad habit and tough to maintain a good one? There's so much to do and so little time. You have a purpose and destiny to which you are to walk in amid the many demands along the way which do not diminish just because you know you have an anointing beyond your present circumstance. You still must go to work and be your best. You still must plan and prepare meals, do laundry, cut the lawn, feed the cat on time, walk the dog twice and sing to the goldfish. Is there any time left for yourself? Is there enough time left to cultivate and nurture the relationship with God that your soul desires? Only you can answer that question, and you must answer the question

– and the sooner the better. Time management is a make or break thing. If you don't manage your time you'll always find yourself trying to find time to pray; time to get it in, rushing to get a quick prayer in just before the presentation, or the meeting and hope that God gives you favor so you won't embarrass him or yourself. Or worse yet, walk away with that sick feeling or regret that comes from knowing you didn't do your best.

Design your prayer life in a way that works for you, early morning before the sun rises and the busyness of the day prevails upon your mind, or evening after the rush of life has settled. Choose a time that best fits your lifestyle and be consistent. Consistency is essential. You can imagine, if you'd like, that being consistent allows God to know what time to expect you to enter into his gates with thanks giving and into his courts with praise. The truth is consistency is more vital for your spiritual health than it is for God. He already knows when to expect your presence. Whether random or regular, God already knows your ETA (exact time of arrival) in the throne room of God. It isn't about keeping God waiting and hoping that today you'll come. It's about your need to be there; to be in the presence of the one who refuels your engine, renews your strength, restores your joy and puts back together the broken pieces that life has caused. It's about being in the presence of the one who clarifies your vision, wipes your tears, and encourages you forward when weariness calls you back. Maintaining consistency says being in the presence of God is a priority. You don't need a book or seminar to tell you how to set your priorities. You know what the priorities are in your life.

You can't fake the anointing!

Your spirit that so depends on fresh anointing is stronger with a consistent personal prayer meeting. Strength and power[vvv] are drawn from the Holy Spirit, and delighting in the presence of

[vvv] Psalm 62:11

God. Delighting in God's presence is just being happy to be there. Beloved, you can't fake the power necessary for the daily strength to get you where God wants you to be; and you can't fake the anointing necessary for the effective use of the power. You must begin with a relationship with the one who is/and has the power and authority, who'll anoint you with more of himself as you grow in that relationship through prayer.

Have Regular Face Time with God

There are days when everything in your world clicks together in perfect time. Traffic is moving smoothly, calm atmosphere on the job, scriptures keep coming to mind; even the nondescript elevator music is blessing you. It's like God has the universe speaking to you on his behalf. You pause in prayer asking God to give you discernment and direction and suddenly you feel the project or the task ahead belongs to you. You are "the man" or "the woman" of the moment. GLORY!!! Other days the world seems flat. You feel so desperate that you'll crack open a Chinese fortune cookie for a motivating thought. Maybe you've been too busy answering everyone's call, meeting everyone else's needs and your spirit is just simply exhausted. The dry, barren and empty times are those when the Spirit of God draws you to green pastures, desiring to lead you beside the still waters so that he can restore your soul.[www]

The Bible speaks of principalities[xxx] and powers and spiritual wickedness in high places.[yyy] A principality as it relates to our interest here is an order of angels, transcending or superior to the physical world in conflict with God. There's a spirit realm around you that you can't see. So, what you're

---

[www] Psalm 23

[xxx] Principalities: territories, countries, domains within a larger kingdom or government

[yyy] Ephesians 6:12

dealing with is a small group of entities with limited power that can mess up things in a big way if you don't protect yourself using the greater power, the Holy Spirit, through the powerful medium of prayer.

You don't go through the day thinking about being in active warfare and under attack unless something's going wrong, plans didn't work out, a loved one dies, a disease comes, kids acting crazy. Prayer becomes an intense concern in difficult times. In the heat of the battle prayers are effective. You cut through the fluff when you're on the battle ground of prayer. The fact is, spiritual warfare is going on 24/7. That's real time, right now time. Praying real time is praying without ceasing.[zzz]" Even when you're in a good space and blessings are overtaking you, put a reminder on your smart phone that there's a plot against you and God's purpose for you. Don't take your eye off the ball. Don't let your guard down. Amid your praise and thanksgiving, pray for protection against what you can't see. Ask for wisdom to handle the onslaught yet to come.

This isn't to suggest that a disciplined prayer life is an insurance policy against dry times. It is not. But it is an assurance and reassurance as you step up to the responsibilities to which you are assigned, the Holy Spirit will do his job in spite of how you feel. A disciplined prayer life keeps your storehouse of assurance filled. There's power in the Name of Jesus and the Holy Spirit releases that power as you spend time in the presence of God.

Pray Wisely

In 2nd Chronicles 1, Solomon, is in a good place. He was walking in God's promise to David that he, his son, would

---

[zzz] I Thessalonians 5:17

be his successor as King of Israel, a very large kingdom. He had thousands of commanders and hundreds of judges under his leadership. He was a worshiper, wealthy, well liked, and had the favor of God. When God appeared to Solomon asking him what he would ask of him, Solomon did three things:

1. He acknowledged God's great mercy and lovingkindness toward his father, David. (Past)

2. He acknowledged that God had kept his promise to make him successor to the throne, entrusted with the leadership of the great number of people who belonged to God. (Present)

3. He asked for wisdom and knowledge to lead God's people justly. (Future)

Clearly God was impressed with Solomon beyond the fact that he was David's son. Solomon's character was reflected in his prayer. God not only granted the wisdom and knowledge Solomon asked for, but riches, possessions, and honor, such as none of the kings who were before him or after him. Solomon prayed in the good times and God made provisions for his future. The point is to be disciplined in your prayer life and to pray wise prayers.

Auto Correct

Of course, we don't always know what to pray for as we should. At times, our judgement may be cloudy, our flesh may be in the way. Maybe our best understanding falls short of the will of God. God created a patch for that. Better yet, he designed Auto Correct. The Holy Spirit will auto correct your prayers.[aaaa]

[aaaa] Romans 8:26-28

Three Things to Pray for:

1. A Teachable Spirit

Re-read the 5th Secret, Always Have a Teachable Spirit. This is contrary to basic human nature. We like to do it our way.

Prayer: *Heavenly Father, give me a teachable spirit. I acknowledge that it doesn't come naturally and I will miss your best for me without it. Help me to receive wisdom that will take me to the higher level for which you've created me to be. Help me to discern, sift, and embrace what's for my good. Amen*

2. A Mentor

There are people whom you admire, smart people, successful people, people at the top of their game in their professions. Perhaps they're even accessible. Secular wisdom offers many "how to's" in choosing a mentor; what to look for, things to consider, etc. Some even say you don't choose your mentor, but that your mentor chooses you. The rules, however, in the Kingdom realm are different. You don't choose your mentor; God chooses your mentor. He created you with a purpose in mind. He knows what it will take to get you to your purpose. He'll bring the right people at the right time to get you to your destiny. It's a match made in heaven and orchestrated by the Holy Spirit on earth. No matter how incredibly gifted you may be, you cannot go it alone. Moses had Jethro,[bbbb] Samuel

---

[bbbb] Exodus 18: 1, 6-27

had Eli,[cccc] Elisha had Elijah,[dddd] Ruth had Naomi,[eeee] Mary had Elizbeth,[ffff] Paul had Barnabus, to name only a few.

The Kingdom of God has not been awaiting your arrival. Others have come this way before you. This is simply your time in the plan of God. You don't know how long your time will be and surely you want it to be the best it can be. Open your ears to hear the experiences of others. A mentor will share their experiences as well as what they've observed. Open your heart to know wisdom. A true mentor will share from a heart of love for their purpose and for those who are committed to the purpose God has designed for them. Open your mind to thoughts other than your own. A mentor will encourage you in the good times, in the rough times, and at all times. A mentor will undergird you in prayer, affirm and find joy in the work of God in you without envy or jealousy.

Prayer: *Heavenly Father, send a mentor that I'll recognize and receive; a person whose wisdom I can trust, in whose counsel I can have confidence; whose journey I respect. Send that person who's seasoned in the same or similar destiny; a person who can keep me grounded and help me to keep my head on straight. Amen*

---

cccc 1 Samuel 3

dddd 2 Kings

eeee Ruth 1:7-18; Ruth 2:17-3:6; Ruth 4:13-17

ffff Luke 1: 39–56

3. A Micah Mindset

But he's already made it plain how to live, what to do, what God is looking for in men and women. It's quite simple: Do what is fair and just to your neighbor, be compassionate and loyal in your love, and don't take yourself too seriously – take God seriously.[gggg]

People will put you on a pedestal. Fight that with all your might. You can't really change the perceptions people have. Often their perceptions are reflections of what they need. But you can control yourself. Never lose sight of your humanity. Hold onto your sense of compassion and mercy. Ruthlessly fight the temptation to be judgmental.[hhhh]

In the poem "If" by Rudyard Kipling he says walk with kings but don't lose the common touch. (paraphrase). Despite your call be able to step down from your seat at the head table and sit with someone who's seated alone. Speak up for those who have no voice. Use your influence to make right things happen.

There are jobs, positions, callings that will have you seated at the king's table but always remember how you got there. You're there because God opened doors for you to be there. You're there because God caused you to be favored in the sight of the powers that be so that you can wisely speak truth to power with prudence. You're there because he trusts you to speak fairly, justly, and compassionately from a heart of mercy, on behalf of his people unconditionally loved and valued. He trusts you to represent him among kings and queens. He sets you in high places so that you can have a better view of the landscape of life, the bigger picture, the long view which allows you to see the intersection of love and truth and to lift the Word

---

[gggg] Micah 6:8 (MSG)

[hhhh] Galatians 6:1

of God off the page in a way that others will only know through their observance of you.

Prayer: *Heavenly Father, give me the courage to have Micah's mindset, to do what is fair and just to my neighbor, be compassionate, loyal in my love, and never judgmental.*[a] *If I have any influence, let me use it to make the right things happen. Amen*

Prayerfully Ponder

1. What's the most important area of your life that needs prayer?

2. List at least five reasons to have a mentor.

3. What are the three main principles in Micah 6:8?

NOTES

NOTES

***Therefore**, since we are surrounded by such a huge crowd of witnesses to the life of faith, let us strip off every weight that slows us down, **especially the sin that so easily trips us up**. And let us run with endurance the race God has set before us.*

— Hebrews 12:1, 2

Secret # 10

Know Your Demons

Because They Know You

THE GOAL OF THIS DISCUSSION ISN'T TO TEACH demonology, amuse, or frighten you in any way. The purpose, as with each discussion, is to give you substantive thoughts to ponder; thoughts that will nudge you to walk watchfully and steer you toward excellence on your journey to your amazing destiny. This secret is particularly important because in the busyness of life, juggling responsibilities, and giving the sincerest effort to honor everything you do with excellence, things can easily be overlooked or their detriment underestimated. You can't afford to overlook anything when it comes to fulfilling God's plan for your life. You are fearfully and wonderfully made. There isn't anyone on the planet like you. God was meticulous in creating you. The bible used the analogy of the potter and the clay in two places expressly speaking of the thoughtful and deliberate attention the potter gives to the clay.[iiii]. You didn't just happen. There was intention and purpose in your being born, the era, the

You are intentional

[iiii] Jeremiah 18; Romans 9

nation in which you were born, your race, complexion, height, weight, socio economic location, parentage; everything that concerns you was intentional for the part you play in God's eternal plan.

To know that you're intentional, that you have meaning and purpose, that you were a forethought and not an afterthought, that you are this and not that, is empowering. When you think about it, it makes you want to put your head up and your shoulders back and feel good about yourself and your possibilities.

BUT! Just as the angels know you and rejoice over you, and there is joy in the earth over you, not every entity is committed to the success of your spiritual purpose. Remember, you are on purpose for a purpose. Everyone isn't cheering God or his plans. The best way to get to him is to get to you. Sometimes we help that along and that's really what this secret is about.

In the Beginning, God

At the very moment you drew your first breath and those present laid their eyes on you marveling at what a beautiful baby you were, at that twinkling of time, your earthly life story began its chronicle on the pages of eternity. No one comes into the world as a blank slate, but that wonder filled moment at the birth of a new life does not disclose that this tiny little person already has a history. At birth, emerging from the womb was a manifestation of God's imagination. You were new to your mother and the rest of the human race but you were not new to the universe or, more specifically, you were known by God.

Paul speaks of your presence in the consciousness of God, being loved and chosen in Christ before the foundation of the world;[jjjj] predestined to be conformed to the image of Christ.[kkkk] You were there somewhere in eternity past and you were fully known by God. That's the spiritual reality. In the beginning, God … from which you must mark your beginning, your history, your spiritual ancestry. Even if you don't know the names in between you must mark your beginning with God. David speaks of God's awareness and very intentional "hands on" as you were in your mother's womb,[llll] so there was never a time that you weren't connected with God even before earthly life began. That's an awesome thought. Being with God in eternity past and down through the corridor of time to the moment of your birth proves the point revealed made in the 2nd Secret, you were not an OOPS!

As briefly referenced in the 6th Secret, contrary to The Tabula Rasa,[mmmm] the blank slate theory of human development, we now know babies aren't born as blank slates on any level. Babies come into this world with volumes of code and genetic predispositions written on their DNA. At times, we're fortunate enough to see personality traits and exceptional gifts passed from one generation to the next. Other times you look at a person and wonder where that particular gift or behavior came from. Often giving careful ear to the elders will reveal information or secrets that connect the dots. Whether apparent, it's all there somewhere.

So it is when you step forward to move into the arena of your destiny. It's like a new birth. Enthusiastic, humbled and thankful, but never blank. There's volumes written on the DNA of your life history that you bring on the journey. Whether you step into the journey of your destiny at 18 or 80 you don't step up alone. Howbeit, visible or invisible, with you are the people

---

jjjj Ephesians 1:4
kkkk Romans 8:29
llll Psalm 139:13-16
mmmm The Tabula Rasa (blank slate) theory of human development, credited to English philosopher, John Locke and Swiss philosopher Jean-Jacques Rousseau

and their impact on your life, their thoughts and interpretations that have passed down and either shaped or influenced your you in some way. You bring your past with you, the experiences of your childhood and beyond, your perceptions and your realities, the vestiges of your life. You bring interpretations of the world around you, trials and tribulations, successes and failures, ideologies, philosophies, superstitions, doubts, and fears. You bring every insult that hurt you, every affirmation that encouraged you, opinions and beliefs that find their authenticity not in the academy but oral history. All of it matters, the good, the bad, the ugly; everything matters because it all culminates into the authentic you. Every experience is like the stroke of a paint brush on the canvas of your life.

The Good
The Bad
The Ugly
Everything matters

In the Delivery Room

At the birth of a child there are at least a few people present in the delivery room associated with the birth, each having a specific role; the medical professionals and whomever they allow to witness the birth, and, of course, the mom. This is the visible crowd, but in the spirit realm there are others present. Paul speaks of the spiritual warfare wherein principalities, powers, rulers of darkness, and spiritual wickedness in high places,[nnnn] referring to a highly-organized military in the spirit realm that targets for attack the children of God. If you read too quickly you'll miss what's between the lines. In any warfare, there's strategy. The efficacy of the enemy's strategy or plan of attack is dependent upon the amount and quality of knowledge obtained about the target of attack. In other words, the more

[nnnn] Ephesians 6:12

knowledge the enemy collects about you the better the chances of his victory over you throughout your life.

What better strategy for the enemy to get to know you then to assign "spiritual stalkers" to meet you as soon as possible, at the moment of birth, stay with and watch you grow. They don't have to do or say anything to you, just take note of your proclivities, watch the habits and appetites you develop. Then at opportune times the enemy can introduce temptations based on the knowledge obtained by just watching and waiting. There's no guest work on the part of the enemy. He knows what will tempt you and what will not. Don't make the mistake in thinking there's good or bad luck involved or things just happen. That thought, too, is a trick of the enemy. He plays a well-designed game of strategy. He's been honing it since he was kicked out of heaven. He's good at it. Just like in football, he's studied your playbook and he's got his own.

The problem isn't
the forbidden
snack;
but the hunger
within

The battleground of decision is the mind. Warfare, the struggle to do what we know is right takes place in the mind. Paul, in Romans 7,[oooo] presents an airtight argument when he talks about the war between the flesh and the spirit. Some interpret this to support the lame excuse, "The devil made me do it," but that isn't at all the tenet of his thought. He clearly states that intellectually he knows what's right. He's simply describing the difficult in making the mental assent to do what the mind knows is right. The mind is always at war with feelings and emotions. We're all familiar with that imagery of the demon on one shoulder and the angel on the other, both talking in your ear trying to persuade you to take their suggested action. No matter how good the case each of them make, the decision to act is an intellectual assent. Don't be fooled by emotions. No

oooo Romans 7:15:25

Strength of the Mind

Philippians 2:5 Let this **mind** *be in you, which was also in Christ Jesus:*

Romans 12:2a And be not conformed to this world: but be ye transformed by the renewing of your **mind,**

Romans 14:5c Let every person be fully persuaded in their own **mind.**

2 Corinthians 8:12a For if there be first a willing **mind,**

2 Corinthians 9:2 For I know the forwardness of your **mind,**

2 Timothy 1:7 For God hath not given us the spirit of fear; but of power, and of love, and of a sound **mind.**

Philemon 1:14 But without thy **mind** *would I do nothing; that thy benefit should not be as it were of necessity, but willingly.*

1 Peter 1:13a, b Wherefore gird up the loins of your **mind,** *be sober*

matter how strong their pull, how intense the desire, how deep the ache, the decision to act one way or another rests solely with the mind. The Bible is very clear about the role the mind plays.

The mind is receptive to subtle suggestions and the enemy knows that. Your mind is particularly receptive when you're tired, weary, lonely, sad, disappointed, feeling defeated, …

The use of questions is a great way to get your mental attention. "Aren't you tired of being lonely?' "Don't you think if things were going to change they would have by now?" "You're stuck, what are you going to do?"

With questions that evoke doubt and fear, those seeds planted firmly in your mind, exploiting your hunger, now the enemy can suggest solutions. Everyone's been there at one time or another. For the purposes of this short consideration, it's not about whether you took the bait.

The question is, "Do you recognize the bait as bait?" Do you recognize the vacuum or the temporary hunger that would urge you to eat something you really don't like? The problem isn't the forbidden snack, it's the hunger within. When you're hungry you'll eat that which you don't like just to ease the pain.

Your "Pet Demon"

A pet demon is just like any other pet. It's something you have in your life because you like it. It fulfills some need you have. You make provisions for it; protect and defend it. You may agree that you shouldn't have it but you do.

> Watch out for that little "pet demon" you keep

The enemy and demons are portrayed as big ugly fire breathing dragons, or an ugly dude with horns, a red suit and a tail, or really ugly nasty monstrous looking rascals that run around hiding in closets and under the bed. Who in the world would listen long enough to be tempted or lured in by something like that.

Neither are those images consistent with the description of Lucifer in scripture.[pppp] Nevertheless, the physical descriptions of demons aren't nearly as important as their alluring nature. Watch out for those darling little demons that suck you in. Watch out for those demons that have become so

Therefore, since we are surrounded by such a huge crowd of witnesses to the life of faith, let us strip off every weight that slows us down, **especially the sin that so easily trips us up.** *And let us run with endurance the race God has set before us.*

Hebrews 12:1

---

pppp Ezekiel 28:12-14

familiar that you don't mind them being around. Watch out for the one(s) that has been around so long that it's become a part of your landscape. Watch out for those demons that seem harmless. You know them. Watch out for that one that you like, that little "pet" demon you have, the one you keep secretly. It's quiet, seems harmless and under control. Watch out especially for that one.

The text clearly says there's a sin which easily trips us up. It tells us to strip it off. KJV tells us to lay it aside. If the Bible says to do it, then it's possible to do, if not by will power, then with the help of the Holy Spirit who is always available. If you can lay it aside, then you know what it is. You're familiar with the sin that gets you every time but for some reason you hold onto it.

This is a nudge. The sin that so easily trips you up could be something as huge as road rage or something you don't consider to be a sin at all, like getting really annoyed when someone habitually doesn't return your call or text, or you go straight to pissed when you see someone spit on the sidewalk. You may have that little feel good demon, the pet spoken of earlier. Strip it off, lay it aside,[qqqq] throw it off.[rrrr] Whichever translation you choose to use, the imperative is offensive action is required on your part to get rid of it. You can't cast it off and take it with you at the same time. Once you've cast it off, then it's behind you; it's in the past. Paul speaks up saying, forget about it, and aggressively move on.[ssss] Know this, a demon is a demon, no matter how subtle, cute, friendly it is or how long it's been with you. It's still a demon and it isn't harmless.

Finally, this thought. Earlier this section mentioned the things you bring with you to any situation, the diverse vestiges of your life. Initially that might bring to mind work related situations, but this includes personal relationships as well. In

---

[qqqq] KJV

[rrrr] NIV

[ssss] Philippians 3:14

fact, in any situation where people are involved, relationships are at work regardless of how personal or impersonal they may be. You bring your entourage of demons and everyone else brings theirs. In business or social settings, you can see how the room can be quite crowded even if there's only three people in the room. Be aware of that. Be so aware that it causes you to deal with your demons even if others don't deal with theirs. Get yours under control so that they don't control the environment. It is not in the purview of this book to discuss interpersonal relationships. That's for the relationship experts to deal with but it would be irresponsible not to bring your attention to the fact that in personal relationships you need to be aware of your demons. They don't leave you because you've fallen in love. If you don't deal with them, you'll have your demons and your partner will have theirs running amuck in your life. Just an FYI.

Prayerfully Ponder

Here are 10 <u>somewhat</u> subtle, not readily visible demons. Do you know of others?

1. Procrastination
2. Mediocrity
3. Narrowmindedness
4. Inflexibility
5. Competitiveness
6. Laziness
7. Cussing
8. Lack of focus
9. Porn & Peep Shows
10. Worthless companions

1. Do you have a pet demon? If so, what is it?

____

____

2. Some demons have become so familiar that you don't mind them being around. Describe that situation.

____

____

____

3. Some demons have been around so long that they've become a part of the landscape. What effect do they have, if any?

____

____

____

THE TOP 10 SECRETS OF AWFULLY AWESOME PEOPLE

1st	YOU'RE ALREADY AWESOME	Release your best self
2nd	BE YOUR AUTHENTIC SELF	Be not guilty of "Identity Theft"
3rd	KEEP YOUR HEAD ON STRAIGHT	Nurture your mind with great thoughts, for you will never go any higher than you think. - Benjamin Disrael
4th	TRAVEL LIGHT	Unpack regularly. Keep only what you need.
5th	ALWAYS HAVE A TEACHABLE SPIRIT	Accept wisdom
6th	CHOOSE YOUR INNER CIRCLE WISELY	You are the average of the five people with whom you spend the most time
7th	WATCH YOUR MOUTH	Watch your mouth!
8th	FLEE JEALOUSY & ENVY	You can be a victim or an offender.
9th	STAY LINKED TO THE CLOUD	Make prayer your Homepage.
10th	KNOW YOUR DEMONS	Because they know you!

NOTES

ABOUT THE AUTHOR

CL LAWRENCE, LEADERSHIP TRAINING STRATEGIST, a dynamic Christian communicator best known for her eclectic approach and distinctive gift of discovering contemporary insights in the Biblical stories while maintaining the integrity of the text. She inspires you to think in new ways, take a fresh look at old assumptions that may be holding you back from making real that vision of your best self. Her passion for excellence and outside the box thinking has made her a much sought after conference speaker, and seminar facilitator. EXCITING. THOUGHT PROVOKING. EMPOWERING, are words used to describe her "Boot Camps," and other events. She combines a 12-year tenure in Corporate America with 30+ years of pastoral and church leadership.

A graduate of Cheyney University, Lutheran Theological Seminary and Tony Campolo School for Social Change; Carol is the founder of Lawrence Seminars, Inc., Host of Empowerment Gatherings (worship & networking events); and Teacher/Facilitator of "Women at the Well" (a unique approach to Bible Study for Women Only). A.K.A. "ZseZse," she's the Creator, Host and Producer of the podcast "Jazz Divine; Zse-votions, (devotional CDs & MP3s); and the Blogcast, "Just Thinking."

To book an engagement
Email:
CL@LawrenceMinistries.com
Visit
LawrenceMinisties.com
&
amazon.com/author/cllawrence

LOOK FOR THESE & OTHER TITLES ON AMAZON.COM & KINDLE.COM

VICTORY OVER YOUR ENEMY

THE JEHOSHAPHAT SAGA

(II CHRONICLES 20)

DIAMONDS IN THE ROUGH

ELISHA'S PLAYBOOK

FOR ASSOCIATE MINISTERS

THE STEPS TO GOOD SUCCESS

WALK, DON'T RUN

Priceless & practical wisdom for life & career

A must read if you're just starting out or you know someone who is

Visit
LawrenceMinistries.com
Subscribe & Download your FREE eBook
"Do You!"
Get your copy of
The Ten
Commandments
of Preaching
@ Amazon.com
Email
DrL@LawrenceMinistries.com
C.L. Lawrence
The Ten
Commandments
of Preaching

www.ingramcontent.com/pod-product-compliance
Lightning Source LLC
Chambersburg PA
CBHW051727040426
42447CB00008B/1011

9780997208252